MARK

Sub Title: Key Bible Study Lessons in The New Testament Gospel of Mark

By Jimmy Davis

Jimmy Davis is retired and currently resides near the small town of Swansea, South Carolina. He served as senior pastor at churches in Indiana and South Carolina. Jimmy was educated at Charleston Southern University, The Southern Baptist Theological Seminary, and Trinity Theological Seminary. These writings are written for sermon preparation, personal devotions, and small group Bible study. Each Bible sermon or teaching may contain codes for the large print NIV pew bibles used in many churches today, and each writing may contain material also found in sermons or teachings in various volumes by the author. This book was originally written with an earlier version of Microsoft Word (written from about 1995 to 2005), therefore the writings may contain some codes, extra spaces, and glitches due to the original format used. Please feel free to share any or all of these works with anyone who will be attentive to learning and studying God's Word. May God richly bless you in your ministry and personal Bible study.

INTRODUCTION TO GOSPEL OF MARK

Mark 1:1

The beginning of the gospel about Jesus Christ, the Son of God.

Summary Sentence: Jesus, as the Son of God has come in the flesh to our world teaching with authority to our amazement.

Our study goal is to met and know Jesus through the God inspired writing of Mark.

Mark was the first to write down the events of the life of Jesus.

Mark worked as a missionary with Paul and Barnabas.

This Gospel is the shortest of the 4, but in some ways the most detailed account of Jesus' ministry and miracles.

Mark shows us Jesus as a man of action and authority, and he spends one third of the book telling events of Christ's last week on earth, ending with the death and resurrection of Christ.

According to tradition, this Gospel was composed to satisfy the urgent request of the people of Rome for a written summary of Peter's preaching in Rome.

The Gospel of Mark was written sometime during the period A.D. 65-67.

This gospel is both a message and a man, the man Jesus.

Preparing The Way

Mark 1:1-8

When you don't know where to start, start at the beginning.

That is what Mark does.

He begins his gospel at the beginning.

In verse 1 he says, "The beginning of the gospel about Jesus Christ, the Son of God."

There are three beginnings in the Bible:

1.   In the beginning was God.
2.   In the beginning was the Word.
3.   In the beginning is the Gospel.

It is the beginning of his Gospel.

But it all didn't simply begin here.

In the beginning of creation, God was already speaking of the coming of the One who would crush the head of the serpent.

Then, with the Old Testament prophets, God spoke again concerning the One who would come as the forerunner; one like Elijah: John the Baptist.

So, as Mark's Gospel opens, we find that the stage is almost set for Jesus' ministry to begin.

John the Baptist is already on the scene.

He was there to prepare the way so that the people would be ready to receive the King.

He was a voice crying in the wilderness.

He was God's bulldozer, sent to build a highway to God; to level hills, raise valleys, straighten crooked ways, and smooth the rough places.

His message would be the road on which the Lord would ride in.

When we find John, we find him in the wilderness.

It was not that John couldn't find a place to preach in the city.

God had sent John to preach in the wilderness.

I find this interesting.

You see, in the wilderness is not the wisdom of the world.

Some would say that this was not the wisest move, at least if you were looking at it from a marketing viewpoint.

I mean, how many people could you draw to the wilderness?

Surely the city would be a better place to begin a ministry.

But the wisdom of God is wiser than the wisdom of man.

Today, we like the church in a place where we can go to it, a building where we can worship.

John didn't work that way: he took the message straight to the people; it's a word for us today to do missions and take the word of God to the people.

Not only did the people come, they came to see and hear John the Baptist in droves.

But this raises another interesting question: "Why did they come?"

They came because of the message which was being preached.

We want to focus on the message which John preached.

Let's turn our attention to two aspects of this message: its allure and its authority.

It's Allure

There is no doubt that the people came to John because his message had a deep appeal to them.

They willingly made the trek from the surrounding countryside to hear this strange preacher.

Strange indeed.

He did not live like other men.

The Bible teaches us that he clothed himself in a garment of camel's hair and that he ate locusts and wild honey.

No doubt, some came in curiosity.

But I am convinced that the vast majority were moved by the strange allure of his message.

They were moved for several reasons.

They were attracted to John's message because John spoke to a universal need.

Deep within us all, there is the realization of our separation from God.

While many like to deny the reality of sin, it is still there.

People only intellectually deny it.

In their hearts they feel the burden of it and it presses in on them.

The knowledge of our imperfections is inescapable.

In the midst of all this, we desperately desire freedom.

That is why they came to John. They had a desire to be free.

For that reward, no price would be too high.

So they came, and came, and came.

Out into the hot, dusty, parched desert, they came.

John's message drew them because it spoke to this universal need.

John was dealing with the sin issue openly.

And they wanted to hear what he had to say.

So they came to this desert place, hoping to hear something that would set them free.

Not only did John's message speak to a universal need, but John's message also offered hope.

The word was out.

People were finding relief.

This wild man of the wilderness was preaching and baptizing and they were finding relief.

So they came.

I suppose all of us are attracted by a message of hope.

You see, John did not preach condemnation.

Some have characterized him as harsh and unloving because he told the truth.

This is not so.

It is not unloving to tell the truth.

While he told the truth about their sin, he did not condemn the sinner.

He preached a word of deliverance.

He preached that now the sinner could be free, that we no longer needed to be a second-class citizen.

This was the part of the allure of his message.

It's Authority

Not only did John's message have certain appealing element which attracted the people.

But it also had a certain authority.

He spoke as one who was telling the truth.

He was telling it like it was.

He dealt with issues other preachers were only dancing around.

And in a day when people soft-pedal the truth, it is exceedingly refreshing to find a man who stands for something and will tell you exactly what he believes.

John was such a man.

John's message was one of repentance.

He called the people to turn from their sins.

A change of heart and behavior was required.

There is a great need for true biblical repentance in the church today.

Repentance is necessary, not only to come to Christ; repentance is necessary for Christians to maintain a close relationship with Christ.

Repentance, at its essence, means both a change of mind and a change of behavior.

It means that we turn from our ways because we have been convinced by God that our ways are wrong.

It means that we humble ourselves before God, that we lay down our pride and bow before Him.

Then John called them to publicly acknowledge their repentance by baptism.

The Jews understood baptism well.

They understood far better than many today the symbolic meaning of baptism.

Baptism symbolized the washing away of the past and the beginning of a new life.

It is the symbol of a totally new person coming forth.

It was such a powerful symbol that under Jewish law, the person was considered a Jew.

The first child born after his baptism was called the firstborn son, even though the couple might have had five other sons previously.

But John wasn't baptizing Gentiles.

John was baptizing Jews.

It says, in verse 4, that he was "preaching a baptism of repentance for the forgiveness of sins."

John's baptism indicated that the person had repented and received God's forgiveness, that he was now coming forth a new person in order to live a new life.

It's all a part of repentance.

This kind of open repentance and confession of sin goes a long way toward building a highway for our God.

In true repentance, we pull down the mountains of our pride, we raise up the dashed hopes of fulfillment.

We straighten out the crooked dealings of our craftiness, and the rough places of our nature are made smooth.

This is the beginning of the good news of Jesus Christ, the Son of God.

John's message was also one of forgiveness.

You see, when you repent, you are forgiven.

This is a basic fundamental reality we Christians need to see clearly.

Many of our problems would be solved if only we saw and lived by this truth.

When we are forgiven, God plunges our sins into the sea of forgetfulness and remembers them no more.

We become free from sin and guilt.

We are cleansed by the blood of the Lamb.

We are clean, forever clean, and we need to start to see ourselves that way.

And we need, also, to begin to see others that way as well.

John's message was one of new life in Christ.

You see, John was only the forerunner to lead us to Christ.

He knew that his ministry was one of pointing to the coming Messiah.

That is why he said that he was unworthy to even untie the laces of Christ's sandals.

Untying someone's shoe laces was a job reserved for the lowliest servant.

John saw that his message was only a beginning.

He was only baptizing with water, but there would come One who would baptize with the Holy Spirit.

Jesus would complete what John had started.

John would fade into the background as Christ came into the foreground.

And that was OK by John.

Only Jesus could take us into the Kingdom.

Repentance and forgiveness are only the beginning of God's work in our lives.

John can bring us to God, but only Jesus can take us on with God.

This work can only be done by the power of the Spirit of God.

That is why we need the One who can baptize with the Holy Spirit.

Only as we are filled by the power of the Holy Spirit can we experience new life in Christ.

The good news is that God will fill us with the Holy Spirit.

That is His desire.

That is your destiny.

This is what God intends for your life.

And that is good news.

That is what John was preaching in the wilderness.

That is why the people came.

That is why they still come.

My purpose in sharing this with you today has been simple.

But pointing out the themes of hope, repentance and confession, forgiveness and forgiving sin, release of guilt and fear, and the possibilities of new life in Jesus, it has been my hope that I may touch those needs in you: Needs to be more honest before God; to be humbled before His love for you; to be more open; to be forgiven and forgiving; and to desire to go on with this great God who made all this possible.

So let me ask you, where are you today?

What is your need?

Can you hear the message of John calling to you?

Are you aware of your own inadequacy before God?

Is it your desire to get down to business with God and be honest before him?

John's message is as relevant today as it was then.

Repentance is still the door through which we must walk to find God.

Do you need to receive God's forgiveness?

There are basically two reasons why people fail to receive forgiveness.

The first is that they fail to repent.

But the second is that they fail to forgive.

Jesus was very explicit about this in Matthew 6:14 and 15. He says, "For if you forgive men for their transgressions, your heavenly Father will also forgive you. But if you do not forgive men, then your Father will not forgive your transgressions."

Is there someone you need to forgive today?

Do not let what others have done destroy your life.

Turn loose of that bitterness and allow God to work healing in your life.

John's message calls us to confront and confess our sins; to turn away from it in sincere repentance; to receive God's forgiveness; and most importantly, to look to Jesus.

Perhaps you have a need to simply look to Jesus today.

Perhaps you have a need to draw closer to him.

Like the prodigal son, God will run to meet you.

He will throw His arms around you.

He will forgive you.

He will restore you.

He will keep you as His son or daughter.

Draw close to Him today, and He will draw close to you.

The Baptism and Temptation of Jesus

Mark1:9-13

In the fifth Century AD St. Patrick baptized King Aengus by full immersion.

During the baptismal ceremony, so the story goes, St. Patrick leaned on his sharp-pointed staff, and inadvertently stabbed the king's foot.

After the baptism was over, St. Patrick looked down at all the blood, realized what he had done, and begged the king's forgiveness.

"Why did you suffer this pain in silence" St Patrick asked.

The king replied, "I thought it was part of the ritual."

In the Gospel of Mark, Chapter 1, beginning with verse 9, we find that this is one of the events that all three of the Synoptic Gospels (Matthew, Mark and Luke) describe, and was obviously an actual event that the Early Church saw of great importance.

Mark's Gospel gives us the briefest details.

Matthew fills out the story a little bit more:

John the Baptist has been summoning people everywhere to repent and be baptized, and Jesus, amongst others, responds by being baptized.

But have you ever wondered

Why did Jesus need to be baptized?"

Does Jesus, the Incarnate Son of God need to repent?

Matthew's account gives us a clue why Jesus was baptized.

In that account we read that John the Baptist at first refused to baptize Jesus, because John felt unworthy.

However Jesus said:

"Let it be so now; it is proper for us to do this to fulfill all righteousness."

What did Jesus mean?

By submitting to baptism, Jesus acknowledged God's claim on Him, as on others, for total consecration of His life and His holiness of character.

I believe there are three reasons that Jesus was baptized.

1. The first reason that I believe Jesus was baptized is that His baptism was a sign of His complete dedication to following the will of God.

For everyone else who came to John for baptism, this required a change in direction – hence the call for them to turn to God.

But for Jesus, baptism was simply a public declaration of His love of God the Father and that He was following the will of God in His life.

You will recall Jesus words in the Garden of Gethsemane, when He knew that He was going to die on the Cross, He prayed: "Father if you are willing, take this cup from me; yet not my will but yours be done" (Luke 22:42).

It was the ultimate submission to the Father's will – to go to the Cross for our sakes – to reconcile us to the Father.

Jesus' baptism was a public declaration of His commitment to God the Father.

But Jesus baptism was more:

2. The second reason Jesus was baptized was it announced the beginning of Jesus' earthly ministry.

John the Baptist and God the Father confirmed Jesus' unique calling publicly.

Jesus baptism was a consecration for His earthly ministry.

And perhaps you will remember God the Father saying something similar at the Transfiguration.

Then a cloud appeared and enveloped them, and a voice came from the cloud: "This is my Son, whom I love. Listen to him!" (Mark 9:7).

3. The third reason Jesus was baptized was as an example to us.

Jesus taught His followers that they needed to be baptized – and here He is giving a firm lead by His example.

The Great Commission in Matthew 28 reads as follows:
Go therefore and make disciples of all nations, baptizing them in the Name of the Father Son and Holy Spirit and teaching them to obey everything I have commanded you (Matthew 28:19-20).

We see God the Father's response:

You are my Son, whom I love; with you I am well pleased.

Folks, when God is pleased, nothing else matters.

It reminds me of a story that Jonathan Goforth (1859-1936) the great Canadian missionary in China, used to tell:

Jonathan's father put him in charge of one of the family farms at the age of 15.

He drew special attention to one very large field, which had become choked with weeds.

His father told Jonathan "Get that field clear and ready for planting. At harvest time, I'll return and inspect it."

Jonathan put a lot of time in plowing and re-plowing, sunning the deadly roots and plowing again until the whole field was ready for planting seed.

He then went and purchased the best seed for sowing.

When all was finished, Jonathan invited his father over to inspect the field.

When his father arrived, Jonathan led him to a high spot from which the whole field of beautiful waving corn could be seen.

Jonathan didn't say a word – he only waited for the words: " Well Done."

His father stood for several minutes silently examining the field for any sign of weeds, but there were none.

Turning to his son, he just smiled.

"That smile was all the reward I wanted" Goforth used to say. "I knew my father was pleased.

So it will be if we are faithful to the trust our heavenly father gives us."

Temptations in Life

Mark 1:12-13
Luke 4: 1-14

There is a story told about a little boy in a grocery store that I think illustrates the nature of temptation.

The boy was standing near an open box of peanut butter cookies.

"Now, young man," said the grocer as he approached the boy.

"What are you up to?"

"Nothing," replied the boy.

"Nothing!" "Well it looks to me like you were trying to take a cookie."

"You're wrong, mister, I'm trying not to!"

That's temptation!

In these two short verses in Mark, Jesus meets the master of temptation.

In this story we will see the general kinds of temptation that our adversary--Satan is still using against us.

This temptation of Jesus came directly after He was baptized.

What a spiritual high—immediately after baptism.

You will discover that testing will often come on the heels of a spiritual high point in your life.

It also came at time of physical weakness; Jesus had not eaten in 40 days.

Temptations often come when we are in a weakened state physically or emotionally, when we are exhausted, and emotionally spent.

Third, this temptation came to Jesus when he was alone.

We are the most susceptible to temptation when we are alone.

The temptations of Jesus had to be real for the consoling truth of Hebrew 4:15 to be true: "For we do not have a High Priest who cannot sympathize with our weaknesses, but was in all points tempted as we are, yet without sin."

To sympathize with us, Christ had to have fully experienced the Devil's temptations!

The devil is well aware that God exists, and I don't think that he expends a great deal of effort trying to dissuade us from a belief in God.

His basic strategy is to make us believe that God can't be trusted.

Satan entered into the Biblical picture at creation in the form of a serpent.

He said to Adam and Eve, "Do you really believe that God is good? He has told you not to eat from that one tree because he knows that the moment you do so you will be as wise as

He is? He is not your friend. He is holding out on you"(Gen. 3:4?).

Satan is suggesting to Jesus that there must be something wrong with the Father's love since "His beloved son" was hungry.

Satan was tempting Jesus to disobey the Father's will by using his divine power for his own purposes.

When Martin Luther was asked how he overcame the devil, he replied, "Well, when he comes knocking at the door of my heart, and asks 'Who lives here?' the dear Lord Jesus goes to the door and says, "Martin Luther used to live here, but he has moved out. Now I live here."

When Christ fills our lives Satan has no entrance.

The Calling Of The First Disciples & Jesus Drives Out an Evil Spirit

Mark 1:14-1:28

Jesus always spoke God's truth with authority!

It has been said that the scribes spoke from authority but that Jesus spoke with authority.

The first words He speaks in verse 15 come as a news flash that the time has come as if to say, "Time's up! You've been waiting how many years for the Messiah to show up? Well, I'm here. And right on time."

God's people can trust in the perfect timing of God.

He may not always come when you want Him, but He is always right on time, and when He shows up it's with supreme authority.

We'll be a lot happier if we remember that sometimes God answers our prayers by saying, "Not yet."

A man once asked God how long a million years was to Him.

God replied, "It's less than a single second of my time."

So the man asked, "And what about a million dollars?"

God replied, "To me, it's less than a single penny."

So the man gathered himself up and said, "Well, God, could I have one of your pennies?"

And God said, "Certainly, my child, hold on just a second."

The timing of God is perfect.

The Lord Jesus came right on time, and He will be right on time when He comes back in His second coming to rule on this earth.

We sometimes wonder that maybe Jesus has forgotten us, but no, He will not be late.

Jesus then trumpets the news that "the kingdom of God is near."

"Near" means, within reach, but not quite in the hand yet.

So when Jesus says, "The kingdom of God is near," He is announcing His authority.

Mark teaches us two important lessons about Jesus. The first is:

1. Jesus Has the Authority to Call Us After Him.

Let's try to imagine the Sea of Galilee.

It's a beautiful fresh-water lake.

The Sea of Galilee is fed by the upper waters of the Jordan River, it is seven hundred feet below sea level, fourteen miles long, and six miles wide.

There's plenty of room for fish, so as we look out across the water, we see many fishing boats sailing upon the lake.

Among those who fished this lake for a living are Simon and his brother, Andrew.

A little further down the water are James and John, sons of Zebedee, who are in the boat.

Like most fishermen, these men have courage, and ability to work together, patience, energy, stamina, faith, and judging by the calluses on their hands, these guys are pretty tough.

But they're not so tough that Jesus is afraid of them.

In fact, according to John's Gospel, Jesus has met them all several months earlier, and His preaching grabbed them by the ears and virtually demanded that they believe in Him as the Messiah.

So on this particular day when Jesus comes walking along the Sea of Galilee, He is able to call these men from their regular occupations and make them His disciples.

"Come, Follow me!" He says.

This is kind of a strange way to start a following.

Usually when a rabbi or a teacher wanted to start a new class he'd wait around in his classroom until the students decided to show up.

Not Jesus.

Jesus goes right up to the water and calls the fishermen right out of their boats.

He tells them He's going to make them become fishers of men.

There is a warning here.

We should see this calling in our own lives as a slow, life-long process.

With a recruiting program like Jesus had, it's really amazing that anybody followed Jesus at all.
But verse 18 tells us; At once they left their nets and followed him.

A few verses down we read that James and John jumped right out of the boat, left their father Zebedee and the hired men in the boat and came straight to Jesus.

This was a once for all action.

No questions asked, no answers offered.

Jesus called, they followed.

The stress in Mark's brief report falls upon the sovereign authority in Jesus' call, and the radical obedience of Simon, Peter, James, and John.

So compelling is the claim of Jesus upon them that all prior claims lose their validity.

Their father, the hired servants, [the family business with] the boat and the nets are left behind, as they commit themselves in an exclusive sense to follow Jesus.

The Gospels present a man who has such charisma that people will sit three days straight, without food, just to hear His riveting words.

Paul wrote, "I count all things to be loss in view of the surpassing value of knowing Christ Jesus my Lord" (Phil. 3:8).

Jesus is just that compelling.

And yet the American Christian's experience is that it takes every last ounce of our will-power to pull ourselves away from what we want to do and follow after Him.

When we finally leave the nets behind, we follow Him around the block, and then we swim right back out to the boat.

One of the reasons we fail again and again and again and again is because we have in our minds the modern day concept of the Prozac Jesus—the mild-mannered Jesus who doesn't really care what I do, and will forgive me anyway if He does care.

American Christians have this way of thinking that we're all registered voters in the politically correct kingdom of God, and if we don't like where Jesus is leading us we can veto His plan.

In His grace God sometimes lets us get away with that for the time being.

But today we have seen the reality of the situation: that the same fiery and determined Jesus that beat the devil down with the cross and freed you from his dictatorship has every right to bring the kingdom of God into your life.

He has the right to zap your brain and force you to serve as His own.

Our King Jesus has every right to put us in chains—in His very own bondage to Himself.

But even with all those rights, rather than lording it over us, He calls out to us, "To Simply Follow Him!"

And then He waits for us to obey with all our heart, freely, gratefully, cheerfully, as though we had no further desire to live life for ourselves because we agree with Paul who says, "I have been crucified with Christ, and it is no longer I who live, but Christ lives in me" (Galatians 2:20).

Romans 12:1 calls us to "offer yourselves as living sacrifices, holy and pleasing to Him."

The infiniteness of God's grace is so clear when we realize that God has made this an option to us.

He gives us the freedom to show our love for Him.

I don't know about you, but that makes me want to follow Him all the more.

His grace to us is even more apparent when we look at the next part of the story where He gives this demon absolutely no options whatsoever.

It's here that Mark gives us a second lesson about Jesus:

2. When Jesus Says Something You Can Count On It Happening.

In this next part of the story we're looking at tonight, we find Jesus teaching in the synagogue.

His new disciples are listening to Him preach, and verse 22 tells us they were amazed by the authority with which He spoke.

Mark put this part of the story here teaching us that it's dangerous to follow Jesus.

But he wants us to see Jesus' authority in action so we won't be so scared.

A demon possessed man is staying here, and we're not sure just how long this he'd been attending services there without anyone knowing.

But on this particular day, he blew his cover as soon as Jesus started teaching.

It must have been Jesus' air of authority that set the demon off.

We have no reason to think that the demon recognized Jesus by His physical appearance because the Bible tells us that Jesus was a regular looking guy.

But as the demon speaks through the man, you can tell he knows what he's up against.

Look at how he talks in verse 24: What do you want with us, Jesus of Nazareth? Have you come to destroy us?

Not "I" and "me", but "we" and "us."

This demon has woven himself through this man so tightly that there's no way he's going to let the poor guy get away from him.

Then he hisses at Jesus, "I know who You are—the Holy One of God!"

To which Jesus says, "Be quiet!" literally, "Be muzzled!"

You see, Jesus didn't need Satan's help telling the world who He is.

He didn't want demonic testimony about Himself any more than these political candidates want the endorsement of Osama Bin Laden.

So He tells the demon to put a muzzle on their mouths and come out of the man, and with that the demon tried one last convulsive attack, but then he had to submit to Jesus' authority and come out of the man.

Verse 27 tells us that everyone there was amazed, buzzing with curiosity.

What's going on here?

A new teaching that does what it says it will do?

Jesus muzzles demonic spirits and sends them packing!

They were surprised because in those days' guys who cast out demons needed some kind of a magical formula to make it happen.

The magician would do some kind of special dance and say, "A-la-peanut-butter and-jelly-sandwiches...in the name of my god with a little 'g', I command you to come out!"

And even then results were hit and miss, almost as if the demons were playing with the exorcist and would sometimes humor him to give a false sense of power.

Jesus needed no magical words.

He said, "Come out of him," and the demon could do nothing else but come out.

When Jesus says something you can count on it happening.

That's how it always is with Jesus.

And it ought to challenge us to give His words all our attention.

So as we read Jesus words together, think them over real good, and then do as He says.

No questions asked, no answers expected.

He calls, we come.

Leaving the nets behind, let's jump out of the boat, and follow Him into this great adventure saying, "Here am I, Lord! I am yours to command! Every part of me belongs to you. I'll leave it all behind for you, my Master, my Savior, my Lord and my God."

The story is told of Alexander the Great who had conquered almost all of the known world.

One day on the warpath, Alexander and small company of soldiers approached a strongly fortified walled city and Alexander raised his voice and demanded to see the king.

When the king arrived, Alexander ordered him to surrender the city and everyone inside to Alexander and his little band of fighting men.

The king laughed, "Why should I surrender to you? You can't do us any harm!"

But Alexander offered to give the king a demonstration.

He ordered his men to line up single file and start marching.

He marched them straight toward a cliff.

The townspeople gathered on the wall and watched in shocked silence as, one by one, Alexander's soldiers marched without hesitation right off the cliff to their deaths!

After ten soldiers died, Alexander ordered the rest of the men to return to his side.

The townspeople and the king immediately surrendered to Alexander the Great.

They realized that if a few men were actually willing to commit suicide at the command of this dynamic leader, then nothing could stop his eventual victory.

Are you willing to be as obedient to the ruler of the universe, Jesus Christ, as those soldiers were to Alexander?

Are you as dedicated and committed?

Think how much power Christ could have in our area with just a portion of such commitment.

The beauty of our Lord Jesus is that unlike Alexander, Jesus loves His followers and wants what's best for them.

He proved this once for all at the cross, where He allowed Himself to be murdered, so that with His blood He could pay the price to free us from Satan himself, that the kingdom of God could come in and we could serve a new King who loves us and rules justly.

One With Authority

Mark 1:21-45

First section includes a review of Mark 1:21-28—Jesus Drives Out An Evil Spirit

Power has always been a fascination to many people.

Our society is intrigued with powerful people.

From the athlete to the entrepreneur; from the physically powerful to the politically powerful, people stand in awe.

For power, many have sold their soul.

People have tried to enhance their own worth by meeting those who have great power and authority.

Some have married for power instead of for the right reasons.

But what the world knows as power and authority is only a corruption of the true power of God.

It has been said that absolute power corrupts absolutely, and that may be true.

If it is, it is because of our corrupt, fallen nature.

If we were not disposed to abuse power, we would not be corrupted by it.

Having the true power of God as his servant is different, however.

It does not corrupt when used by the leadership of the Holy Spirit.

This is what we see in Jesus.

In our text, and in Scripture as a whole, we see, in Jesus, power used as it was intended by God to be used.

We see power used not to swell the ego, but to minister to the people.

We see power used not to call attention to itself, but to attest to the mercy of God, and call people to Him.

In our text, we see the authority of God revealed in Jesus Christ.

Jesus is described in our text today as "One having authority."

This word denotes the right to exercise power.

And in Jesus, we see one who has that right.

But what can we learn from Jesus' use and exercise of power?

He has left us on this earth as His representatives.

He has imparted to us authority and called us to do the "greater works."

But if we would know how to use power without being corrupted by it, we must look at His example.

We can learn much from Him.

Power Personified

Let's turn our attention to the personification of power as it is revealed in Jesus.

When you think of power personified, only one name comes to mind – Jesus Christ.

He is the "One with authority."

The authority of Christ is revealed throughout the Scripture.

Already in Mark, we have seen the authority of Christ revealed.

Here in the first chapter, in verses 12 and 13, we see His authority over the temptation of Satan as He came forth from the wilderness experience, victorious.

And in verses 16 through 20, we see His authority over men, as He called His first disciples and they left all to follow Him.

In Luke's account, when He called the disciples, we have a scene where He asserted His authority over nature in providing the net full of fishes after a long night's toil without a catch.

So, when we come to our passage of Scripture today, which is a short review of where we were last Sunday night and we continue the theme of the authority of Christ.

He is the perfect personification of authority.

The first thing we see is that Christ's authority is greater than the Scribes'.

When Jesus came into Capernaum, He began to teach in the synagogue there.

Verse 22 says that they were amazed at His teaching.

But why were they astonished?

They were astonished because He did not teach as other men of that day taught.

When the Scribes stood up to teach, they always appealed to other authorities besides themselves.

They would say, "According to Rabbi Gamaliel . . . or Rabbi Hillel . . . or Rabbi Shammai . . . or Rabbi so-and-so" and then they would teach.

But they would always appeal to external authorities to substantiate their views.

This is what we still do today.

In order to convince someone of the validity of what we are saying, we appeal to a supposed authority to prove our case.

For instance, if I were talking to you about the proper way to train your children in certain areas of their development, I might appeal to a respected expert like Dr. James Dobson, or someone else like Him.

Or I might say that a certain study done by Drs. So-and-so revealed a certain truth.

The reason I would do that is because if I just said you ought to do this or that, you may question whether I knew what I was talking about.

You may say, "What makes him an authority on this subject?"

And in many cases, you would have good reason for doing so.

I have even heard so-called experts appeal to other so-called experts for their authority.

This is still common practice.

But Jesus did not do that.

He stood up and said, "This is the way it is."

There was no Rabbi So-and-so to get His authority from.

It was simply Jesus' word, period.

But there was power in His word.

I personally believe that what Jesus said rang true to the hearts of those who were listening.

They knew He was right.

And they were astonished at His teaching because it rang true and because He taught with authority.

Jesus Christ has authority.

His authority was greater than the authority of the Scribes.

He had authority to establish truth.

Next, we see that Jesus' authority was greater than Satan's.

Not only was Jesus' authority greater than the Scribes, His authority was greater than Satan's.

What we see revealed here in this passage of Scripture is Christ's authority to deliver the afflicted.

Here, Jesus encounters the demonic work of Satan himself, and casts the demons out.

In fact, this was one of the signs of the coming of the Messiah.

When the Messiah would come, miracles such as healing and deliverance would occur.

In Isaiah 35:5-6 we read, "Then the eyes of the blind will be opened, and the ears of the deaf will be unstopped. Then the lame will leap like a deer, and the tongue of the dumb will shout for joy."

In Jesus' encounter with these demons, we have evidence of Jesus being the Messiah.

And those who saw these things that day could only come to that conclusion.

They saw the power of God being manifested in the man.

By His word, the forces of hell had to retreat.

He spoke and they had to obey.

Here was a man who had authority.

Here was a man who was the personification of power; pure power, but power used not to draw attention to the greatness of the one using it, but power used to the benefit of those in need.

Next, we see that Jesus' authority is greater than sickness.

Read Mark 1: 29-45 In these passages of Scripture, we see that Jesus authority was not only greater than the Scribes', not only greater than Satan, but it was also greater than sickness.

Sickness has been with us since the Fall of Man.

When Adam fell, he brought the entire created order down with him.

The entire universe is running down.

Science calls this the Second Law Of Thermodynamics, or the Law of Entropy, which, simply stated, says that all things are running down, or are subject to the degenerative forces now operative in the universe.

And so it is with our bodies.

We are running down.

We call that aging.

And we will eventually die.

We have not been delivered from that part of the effect of the fall of man.

Saved and lost alike die in the flesh.

That is still part of God's plan for us.

And we also get sick in the flesh.

To some, this is a horrible thing.

But relatively speaking to be sick of spirit is much worse than to be sick of body.

We reveal our earth-bound mentality when we emphasize the physical instead of the spiritual.

Perhaps if more people would seek spiritual healing, their physical problems would be taken care of as well.

But back to our point.

We have physical infirmities, and Jesus has authority over our physical infirmities.

He has the power to heal, and that is what is manifested in these two passages of Scripture we have just read.

With Simon's mother-in-law and with the leper, Jesus manifested His authority over sickness.

He healed them both.

Here was another sign of His being the Messiah.

Here was a sign that the Kingdom of God had broken in on them.

In Christ, we see the perfect personification of power. Revealed in the person of Jesus Christ is absolute power; but also pure power, power used to help others, power used, without the one using it being corrupted.

In Christ we have the perfect example of how to use the power of God.

But, of course, we are not Christ.

We do not have the same degree of authority and power which He manifested.

That is true, but God does desire to manifest His power through us.

God does desire to endue each of us with power so we can minister in His name.

God has made us agents of the Kingdom.

We are His ambassadors.

We are representatives of Jesus Christ.

We, too, can receive the power of God and use the power of God if we come to understand how to do so.

Power Perpetuated

God desires to reproduce His power in us and to use it through us.

Let's turn our attention now to the perpetuation of power as it is received by us.

First, it is important for us to see that the source of power is God.

We see this clearly revealed in the life of Jesus.

The revelation of the power of God in Jesus was evidence of the fact that He was the Messiah.

The power He manifested was God's power.

Jesus Himself said it was so.

Over and over in John's Gospel, Jesus says that the works He is doing are not His works, but the Father's works.

He says that His teaching is, in reality, the Father's teaching, that all He is doing is what He sees the Father do.

Jesus always pointed us to the Father as the source of His power.

In reality, Jesus and the Father are one.

Only God has the kind of power we see manifested in the life of Jesus Christ.

God is the source of all power.

And if we would manifest the power of God, we have to understand that He alone is the source of that power.

The second thing we need to see is that the secret of power is prayer.

Look again at verses 35-39

There is a key here to Jesus' ministry and to the ministry of every effective saint of God.

It is prayer.

Jesus was always stealing away to pray.

In this passage, it says that He rose a great while before day to be alone in prayer.

That is where He communed with the Father.

That is where He received guidance.

That is where He heard the Father speak.

That is where He received the power and authority to act in the name of the Father.

And that is the only place where we will get the authority to act in the name of Jesus.

If He must pray, we must pray.

And if Jesus needed to pray, how much more do we.

Prayer is the secret of receiving God's power.

When God's people begin to pray, God begins to act.

Finally, what is the standard for how we use the power of God?

Of course, the standard is how Jesus used His power.

As He used power, so are we to use power.

And in each case, He was ministering to the needs of others.

He had compassion on the needy.

He cared that the demon-possessed was bound.

He cared that there was suffering.

He wanted to see people set free.

That was His motive and that should be ours.

For Jesus, power was not a show.

So many today seem to make the things of God a show.

It is as if they are calling attention to themselves, saying, "Look who I am."

They advertise the power of God to gain a crowd.

But, this is not what Jesus did.

In fact, He told them not to tell of these things.

Why?

Because He did not want the curiosity-seekers.

He did not want those who only wanted something for themselves without a commitment to God.

He knew they would not last.

And those who came that way didn't.

They left Him, and they still do.

Many today come to meetings seeking a blessing, and even when they get one, you never see any real commitment in their lives.

God is just a blessing machine to some.

He is someone to come to "to get what I need."

And incidentally, that is why so many do not get what they are asking for, whether it's healing or some other thing.

We must never want to see the power of God working in a meeting just to see it.

God does not want to perform for us.

He did not perform for the Devil by turning the stones into bread, and He will not perform for us so we will believe He is there.

But He will as He did here, perform His works so we will be healed and delivered and made whole for His sake.

And the reason is because He cares for us.

He uses His power, His authority, to minister to others, and so should we.

We should have a desire to see people ministered to.

The first thing we think about should not be ourselves, but those who are in need – the lonely, the poor, the hurting, that in prison, the sick, the afflicted.

It's sad that some do not want to soil their sanitary hands with such people.

But that was not Jesus' way.

In the case of the leper, Jesus reached out His hand and touched Him.

Now, this was unheard of.

A leper was a horribly unclean person.

Their flesh was full of disease. It was literally rotting off their bones.

They were required to walk around and cry "Unclean! Unclean!

Someone would be out of their mind to touch a leper.

You might get leprosy.

How could anyone touch such a foul person?

Well, Jesus did.

And He made a point of doing it.

Why?

So we would have an example of what we would do.

He could have just spoken to him and healed him but He didn't.

He touched him.

And we need to touch others in every way.

It is nothing but selfishness to do otherwise.

Oh, you may call it prudent, or wise.

But we are to be pitied if we do, because we have deceived even ourselves.

And we have condemned ourselves to selfish quenching of the Spirit in our lives.

But as we do reach out and touch those who are in need, we begin to be enlarged in our Spirit.

The blessing of God is attendant upon such action.

The joy of the Lord flows into our souls and our spirits are lifted up.

That is how Christ used His power – for others.

And that is how we should use the gifts He gives us.

Jesus has given us a real insight into His authority and power and how to use it.

It is for our instruction that we may follow in His steps.

But it may only come when we give ourselves to Him, to seek His face in prayer, and to seek to use what we have for His will for those who need Him.

We are His hand to touch them today.

As I look around this church, I am made aware of the great number of you who have been blessed by God.

You have not only blessed materially and financially, you have been blessed with many gifts and abilities, talents and capabilities.

There is great potential here to be used for the Kingdom of Christ.

What are we doing with it?

The Scripture says that we are to be good stewards of the grace of God.

How are we exercising that stewardship?

The authority of Christ has been imparted to us.

The gifts of God have been given to us.

There is more, plenty more, where all of that came from.

What are we doing with it?

We have been given much.

But to whom much is given, much is required.

Are we using our time, our talents, our money and our gifts for the sake of the Kingdom: Are we engaged in Kingdom work?

Do we have a burden for those who are hurting, for those who are lost?

How are we using the authority and power that we possess?

It is not my desire to do anything but be an encouragement to you.

But I must constantly hold before you the inescapable consequences of a lack of attention to Kingdom work.

If we, as a people, are going to really make a difference in the lives of others; if we are going to be the dynamic, aggressive, power-filled church that makes a difference, we must actively seek out ways to touch the lives of others.

God has called us by His marvelous grace.

He has made us a bright, shining beacon of hope to a struggling world lost in the darkness.

We must never take for granted the glorious riches of His grace deposited here in our midst.

We are blessed.

Let's use that blessing to bless others.

SERMON # 669

"NO ONE & EVERYONE IS `NUMBER ONE'"

READ MARK 1:40-45   (JESUS' HEALING OF ONE WITH LEPROSY)

READ LEVITICUS 13:1-3

WHEN PERSONALIZED LICENSE PLATES WERE FIRST INTRODUCED, THE DEPARTMENT OF MOTOR VEHICLES RECEIVED OVER 1,000 REQUESTS FOR THE NUMBER "ONE".

THE STATE OFFICIAL WHOSE JOB IT WAS TO APPROVE THESE REQUESTS SAID, "I'M NOT ABOUT TO ASSIGN NUMBER "ONE" TO SOMEONE AND DISAPPOINT 1,000 PEOPLE.

SO HE ASSIGNED THE NUMBER "ONE" TO HIMSELF!

A LITTLE BOY AND A LITTLE GIRL WERE RIDING A MECHANICAL HORSE IN A SHOPPING MALL.

THE LITTLE BOY, WHO WAS RIDING IN FRONT, TURNED TO THE LITTLE GIRL AND SAID, "IF ONE OF US GETS OFF, THERE WOULD BE MORE ROOM FOR ME."

ORIGINAL SIN ALL BEGAN IN THE GARDEN OF EDEN WHEN THE DEVIL CONVINCED ADAM AND EVE THAT HE HAD FOUND A WAY FOR THEM TO MOVE GOD OUT OF THE "NUMBER ONE" SPOT.

AND WE KEEP LOOKING FOR WAYS TO SUCCEED WHERE ADAM AND EVE FAILED.

WE LOOK FOR WAYS TO BE FIRST ON EVERYONE'S PRIORITY LIST.

WE LOOK FOR WAYS TO BE FIRST IN LINE.

WE LOOK FOR WAYS TO BE FIRST AT THE CHECK-OUT COUNTER.

WE LOOK FOR WAYS TO BE FIRST GETTING OUT OF THE PARKING LOT.

AND WE LOOK FOR WAYS TO BE KNOWN AS DISCIPLES OF CHRIST WITHOUT FOLLOWING HIS EXAMPLE.

TWO OF THE ORIGINAL DISCIPLES OF JESUS SAID TO JESUS, "TEACHER, WE WANT YOU TO DO FOR US WHATEVER WE ASK OF YOU."

JESUS SAID, "WHAT DO YOU WANT ME TO DO FOR YOU?"

AND THEY SAID TO HIM, "GRANT US TO SIT, ONE AT YOUR RIGHT AND ONE AT YOUR LEFT, IN YOUR GLORY".

IN OTHER WORDS, "WHEN WE GET TO HEAVEN WITH YOU, WE WANT THE TOP SPOT."

"WE WANT TO BE NUMBER "ONE" UP THERE.

JESUS SAID TO THEM, "YOU DO NOT KNOW WHAT YOU ARE ASKING. WHOEVER WOULD BE GREAT AMONG YOU MUST BE THE SLAVE OF ALL. FOR THE SON OF MAN ALSO CAME NOT TO BE SERVED BUT TO SERVE; AND TO GIVE HIS LIFE AS A RANSOM FOR MANY." (MARK 10:38;43-45).

THE GREAT RUSSIAN WRITER, TOLSTOY, WAS WALKING DOWN THE STREET ONE DAY WHEN A MAN IN RAGGED CLOTHES BEGGED HIM FOR SOME MONEY.

TOLSTOY REACHED IN HIS POCKETS FOR A COIN, BUT HE COULDN'T FIND ONE.

HE SAID TO THE BEGGAR, "I'M SORRY, MY BROTHER, BUT I DON'T HAVE ANY MONEY ON ME."

THE BEGGAR SAID, "YOU HAVE GIVEN ME MORE THAN I ASKED FOR. YOU HAVE CALLED ME `BROTHER'".

WE ARE ALL MEMBERS OF THE FAMILY OF GOD.

WE NUMBER IN THE BILLIONS!

WHOEVER WOULD LIKE TO BE GREAT AMONG THEM, MUST FIRST BE THEIR SERVANT.

NO ONE IS "NUMBER ONE" AND EVERYONE IS "NUMBER ONE".

THIS IS JESUS' REMEDY FOR OUR BROKENNESS!

A MAN WALKED INTO A SUNDAY SCHOOL CLASSROOM.

HE LOOKED AROUND AND SAW THERE WAS ONE EMPTY SEAT.

HE SAID TO THE WOMAN SITTING NEXT TO THIS EMPTY SEAT, "IS THIS CHAIR SAVED?"

THE WOMAN LOOKED UP AND SAID, "NOT YET, BUT WE'RE STILL PRAYING FOR IT."

IN THE BIBLE, THE WORD "SALVATION" CONVEYS A MEANING OF RELATIONSHIPS WHICH HAVE BEEN HEALED!

IN OUR PASSAGE WE READ IN MARK, A LEPER CAME TO JESUS BEGGING AS HE CAME ON HIS KNEES: "IF YOU ARE WILLING, YOU CAN MAKE ME CLEAN." (MARK 1:40).

IN THE DAY OF JESUS, LEPERS WERE VERY COMMON.

THERE WAS NO DISEASE REGARDED WITH MORE TERROR AND PITY THAN THE DISEASE OF LEPROSY.

TODAY, WE NO LONGER CALL THIS DISEASE LEPROSY, BUT INSTEAD WE KNOW THIS DISEASE AS "HANSEN'S DISEASE".

THERE ARE THREE KINDS OF LEPROSY!

1.   THERE IS "NODULAR" OR "TUBERCULAR" LEPROSY.

THIS TYPE BEGINS WITH UNACCOUNTABLE PAINS IN THE JOINTS.

DISCOLORED PATCHES APPEAR ON THE BODY. FIRST THEY ARE PINK, THEN THEY TURN BROWN.

THE SKIN BEGINS TO GAIN THICKNESS AND ULCERS FORM ON THE SKIN AND THEY DISCHARGE A FOUL ODOR.

SLOWLY THE SUFFERER BECOMES A MASS OF ULCERATED GROWTHS.

THE AVERAGE COURSE OF THIS TYPE OF LEPROSY IS 9 YEARS; AND IT ALWAYS ENDS IN MENTAL DECAY, COMA AND DEATH.

2.   THE SECOND TYPE OF LEPROSY IS CALL "ANAESTHETIC" LEPROSY.

IN THIS TYPE OF LEPROSY, THE NERVES ARE AFFECTED,

THE INFECTED AREA LOSES ALL SENSATION.

THE SUFFERER MAY NOT REALIZE WHAT HAS HAPPENED UNTIL THERE IS NO PAIN AND NO FEELING WHERE PAIN SHOULD BE AFTER A BURN OR A FALL.

THERE IS DISFIGUREMENT OF THE FINGER NAILS AND THE PROGRESSIVE LOSS OF FINGERS AND TOES.

A WHOLE HAND OR A FOOT MAY DROP OFF.

THE DURATION OF THIS TYPE OF LEPROSY IS FROM 20-30 YEARS.

3.   THE THIRD TYPE IS THE MOST COMMON OF ALL. "NODULAR" AND "ANAESTHETIC" LEPROSY ARE MIXED IN COMBINATION.

THERE WERE MANY PEOPLE WHO SUFFERED WITH THIS COMBINATION TYPE LEPROSY IN PALESTINE DURING THE TIME OF JESUS.

A "PSORIASIS" WHICH IS A DISEASE WHICH COVERS THE BODY WITH WHITE SCALES DISTINGUISHES THIS TYPE.

WITH MEDICAL KNOWLEDGE STILL IN AN EXTREMELY PRIMITIVE CONDITION IN THE DAYS OF JESUS, THE LEPER WAS BANISHED FROM THE FELLOWSHIP AND WERE CONSIDERED SOCIAL OUTCAST.

THEY WERE CONSIDERED TO BE PHYSICALLY UNCLEAN AS WELL AS SPIRITUALLY UNCLEAN.

THEY WERE DRIVEN OUT OF THE COMMUNITY AND REQUIRED TO KEEP THEIR DISTANCE.

THEY HAD TO WEAR BLACK CLOTHES SO PEOPLE WOULD NOTICE THEM.

THEY COULDN'T COME NEAR CHURCH SERVICES AND EVERYWHERE THEY WENT, THEY HAD TO CALL OUT: "UNCLEAN, UNCLEAN, UNCLEAN."

IN OUR STORY TONIGHT, JESUS DOESN'T TELL THE LEPER TO KEEP HIS DISTANCE.

EVEN THOUGH THE LEPER HAD NO RIGHT TO EVEN BE SPEAKING TO JESUS, JESUS DOESN'T ASK QUESTIONS ABOUT HIS MISERABLE CONDITION.

INSTEAD, JESUS DRAWS HIM CLOSE TO HIM.

MOVED WITH PITY, HE REACHED OUT HIS HAND AND TOUCHED THE MAN AND SAID, "I AM WILLING"..."BE CLEAN!"

THE SMALLEST PACKAGE IN THE WORLD IS THE PERSON WHO IS ALL WRAPPED UP IN HIMSELF OR HERSELF.

AFTER HEARING A SERMON ON "PRIDE", A WOMAN APPROACHED HER PASTOR WITH A CONFESSION.

"I FEEL GUILTY", SHE SAID.

"THIS MORNING, BEFORE COMING TO CHURCH, I COMMITTED THE SIN OF PRIDE."

"I SAT FOR AN HOUR IN FRONT OF THE MIRROR ADMIRING MY BEAUTY."

THE PASTOR REPLIED, "MY DEAR, THAT WASN'T PRIDE, THAT WAS IMAGINATION."

NO ONE AND YET EVERYONE IS NUMBER ONE!

"SINCE WE LIVE BY THE SPIRIT, LET US KEEP IN STEP WITH THE SPIRIT. LET US NOT BECOME CONCEITED, PROVOKING AND ENVYING EACH OTHER." (GAL. 5:25).

"CARRY EACH OTHER'S BURDEN, AND IN THIS WAY YOU WILL FULFILL THE LAW OF CHRIST. IF ANYONE THINKS HE IS SOMETHING WHEN HE IS NOTHING, HE DECEIVES HIMSELF. EACH ONE SHOULD TEST HIS OWN ACTIONS. THEN HE CAN TAKE PRIDE IN HIMSELF, WITHOUT COMPARING HIMSELF TO SOMEBODY ELSE, FOR EACH ONE SHOULD CARRY HIS OWN LOAD." (GAL. 6:2-5).

THE CHRISTIAN WHO REMAINS SAFELY WITHIN THE CAMP, REFUSING TO REACH OUT, HAS MISSED THE WHOLE POINT OF THE GOSPEL.

WE ARE ALL LIKE THE LEPER, IN THAT WE ARE ALL POTENTIAL OUTCASTS.

WE ARE ALL VULNERABLE TO THE DISEASE OF FEELING TERRIBLY LONELY AND UNWANTED.

ALLOW GOD'S LOVE FOR YOU TO GIVE YOU A NEW KIND OF STRENGTH BEYOND YOUR OWN STRENGTH.

HE IS READY TO SUPPORT YOU IN ALL YOUR NEEDS.

LET THIS DAY BE A DAY YOU REMEMBER THE JOYS OF BEING LOVED BY GOD.

WE ARE COMMISSIONED BY GOD TO DISCOVER THE REAL MEANING AND PURPOSE OF OUR LIVES THROUGH THE EXPERIENCE OF LOVE FOR GOD AND FOR ONE ANOTHER.

Blessed Are The Flexible

Mark 2:18-3:6

I heard a new beatitude.

Jesus didn't say it, but it is true: "Blessed are the flexible, for they shall not be broken."

It is so easy to become inflexible, isn't it?

Especially as Christians, we find ourselves falling into the trap of legalism.

Because we care about God's Word and about Jesus' commandments, sometimes we write our own little set of standards to which people must conform.

We end up judging everybody by those standards, even when those standards are based more on tradition than Bible.

It is very easy for us to become set in our ways.

This is true not only for individuals, but also for churches.

We quickly fall into certain routines, and after we do a thing for a certain period of time, it becomes sacred.

The routine becomes the right way.

And whenever someone upsets our routine, we are upset.

Ralph Neighbour wrote a book entitled, The Seven Last Words Of The Church.

He defined those words as "We never did it that way before."

Sadly, those are the very words which cause many churches to die.

Inflexibility, the status quo, and legalism – these can be the worst enemies of the Church.

Jesus and His followers upset the status quo.

Oh, I know that there are some who think of Jesus as a mild-mannered man, timid and soft, a kind of Clark Kent.

But that is not the picture we get of Jesus when we read the Gospels honestly.

We see there that Jesus was far from the image some have portrayed him to be.

The Clark Kent turns into the real superman we have all been waiting for because Jesus was a real man in every sense of the word.

And He was a man who stirred up controversy wherever He went.

When He confronted religious hypocrisy, He met it head on and called it what it was.

When He saw traditions made by man in the name of God, He flouted them publicly.

And many who saw it didn't like it at all.

Today, we have a passage in which Jesus deliberately provoked certain groups of religious leaders to challenge the status quo.

Our text reveals areas in which Jesus broke their laws.

In the areas of fasting, and the Sabbath, Jesus did more than ruffle the feathers of these inflexible religionists.

We see in this passage, several events which show Jesus' authority over tradition, His purpose behind transgressing it, and the new tradition He is inaugurating.

There is a message to us about the real meaning of the Law, and about our attitudes toward it, and about the new life God is bringing to those who are open and flexible enough to receive it.

The problem of fasting.

It is found in verses 18 through 20. There was only one day per year required for fasting, and that was the Day of Atonement.

But the Pharisees had wanted to show their piety to both men and God, so they began to fast two times a week.

And they made a great show of it, putting ashes on their faces and appearing in rough clothes before men.

They hoped people would notice their great piety.

But Jesus was not impressed.

And on one of those fast days, He and his disciples were feasting away.

Now, even John's disciples fasted, so the question was put to Jesus why He and His disciples did not observe this tradition.

In His reply, Jesus used the illustration of the marriage feast.

In Israel, marriage was a gala event, even more so than it is in the country.

The bridegroom and the bride did not have a 30-minute service and short reception, and then go off into the night.

Sometimes the feast would go on for a week.

And those who were invited to the feast were exempted from all duty which would lessen their joy in celebrating that occasion.

This, of course, included fasting.

This was the illustration Jesus used concerning Himself - that He was the bridegroom, and that as long as He was present with His disciples, they should feast and be joyful.

That, you see, should be the position of every believer in the presence of the Lord – fullness of joy.

Notice that the action of Jesus centers on a relationship with human beings, instead of on the rules of tradition.

The attitude, however, of the religious Pharisees was to shout, "Keep the tradition!"

To them, tradition was more important than people.

Then, there is the problem of the Sabbath.

In order to understand this, we must see what the Sabbath was supposed to be and what it came to be.

The Sabbath principle was established at creation, when God rested on the 7th day from all His labors.

The Sabbath itself was established in the Law of Moses, which God gave on Mt. Sinai.

He set it apart and said that no work should be done on that day because it was a holy day.

Now, the reason for this was human need.

God knew we needed a day of rest in seven, and He provided that for us.

The Sabbath was, and still is Saturday, the 7th day of the week.

As Christians, we have set apart another day, Sunday, or The Lord's Day, for worship.

It is not the Sabbath.

It is our day, the day of Resurrection.

And the Church has always made that a very special day, but the Sabbath remained a day of rest.

In our passage today, Jesus encounters still opposition concerning the Sabbath.

This is found in Mark 2:23-3-6.

In the first case, His disciples were walking through the grain fields and plucking ears of corn.

Now, this was perfectly legal to do, as long as the traveler did not put a sickle to the grain, he was allowed to pluck the ears of corn by hand for food on his journey.

But this was the Sabbath day, and the Sabbath had become something beset by tradition.

You see, the Pharisees and other religious leaders had felt a need to define what God really meant by "no work," and it went even to the absurd.

For example, it was fine to spit on a rock on the Sabbath, but you could not spit on the ground, because that made mud and mud was mortar, and that was work.

Such were the rules of the Sabbath – rules made by men.

But it had become a burden instead of a blessing for man.

And so, when Jesus was confronted with these rules for the Sabbath concerning His disciples picking grain to satisfy their hunger, He reminded them that in their Scripture, there was evidence of the readiness of God to meet need, as He met the need of David and his hungry men, by allowing them to eat the consecrated Shewbread, which was normally reserved for the priests only.

Jesus gave them the real purpose of the Sabbath as God intended for it to be when He said, "The Sabbath was made for man, not man for the Sabbath."

But it did not end there.

These Pharisees had not seen the truth.

Men of hard hearts many times never see.

Jesus next went to the synagogue on the Sabbath.

And in that place, there was a man with a withered hand.

And even though these Pharisees would not see the truth of His teaching, they were starting to understand Him, because they knew that He would seek out this man with the withered hand in order to help him.

Jesus would not be at the front of the synagogue rubbing shoulders with the honored scholars, but He would seek out the needy.

They were counting on it.

Why?

Did they want to see the end of this man's suffering?

No.

They were counting on it because they wanted to trap Jesus.

What motives!

What hardness of heart!

Mark says that Jesus called the man with the withered hand to Him.

He asked the Pharisees if it was lawful to do good on the Sabbath, as He intended to do, or evil, as they intended in their hearts.

They were silent.

Mark says that He looked on them with anger, being grieved at their hardness of heart.

Then, He healed the man with the withered hand, showing that He cared more for Him than for keeping the rules of man.

He exposed the evil of the Pharisees in doing that, and they hated Him for it.

From that time on, they plotted how to kill Him.

Again, we see the action of Jesus in meeting human need, and the attitude of the religious Pharisees, as they would shout, "Keep the Law!"

But what is the message here?

That tradition is made to be flouted?

That rules are to be broken?

The message is that God is concerned with human need, and so should we be.

The law of love, God's agape love, should govern us.

And where we find real need, we are to minister to it, even if it brings us down in the eyes of the self-righteous in the community.

We may be associated with what they consider the "dregs" of life, but that is where the need is.

They may not dirty their hands with such people, but of such is the Kingdom made; of such were some of you.

To have their attitude is to be like the world.

To be like Jesus, you may have to defy some traditions of your own making.

We must not let our priorities get out of perspective.

When God begins to work, traditions are secondary.

His power to touch human lives is primary.

The Newness of Life

We have focused on the narrowness of law.

Now, let's turn our attention to the newness of life.

In our text, there is the unmistakable message that the Kingdom age is here; that a new way of life has come.

Look at what Jesus is telling us in verses 21 and 22.

No one sews a patch of un-shrunk cloth on an old garment. If he does, the new piece will pull away from the old, making the tear worse. And no one pours new wine into old wineskins. If he does, the wine will burst the skins, and both the wine and the wineskins will be ruined. No, he pours new wine into new wineskins (vv. 21-22)

Jesus is telling us that He has brought with Him an age of new wine.

There is a need for new wine.

New wine is symbolic of new life.

It is the move of God in the midst of His people.

It is the Spirit unleashed with power in the Church.

This is what the Church of Jesus Christ needs in our day – a fresh move of God in her midst.

This is what we need as individual Christians, as well.

The action of Jesus was new wine in their midst.

God was doing something fresh and new.

He has always done that throughout the history of the Church.

There have been various renewals and awakenings, various outpourings and revivals.

And when the Church has responded, God has done a new thing in her midst.

When individuals respond, God pours forth His Spirit upon them.

But not only do we need new wine, we need new wineskins.

The new things of God must be contained in new forms.

The old forms cannot hold them.

Just as in the case of the new cloth sewn on the old garment, in which the new was not pre-shrunk, and would shrink and tear the old, so also this new life of the Spirit would not be compatible with the old forms.

So also is the case of the wineskins.

The old wineskins are old forms.

And in the context, forms in the tradition of men.

They are stretched out, hard and brittle.

If you were to put new wine in them, as it fermented it would give off gases and burst the old brittle wineskins and all would be lost.

Much of what they had done to that point consisted of serving in the Temple.

It was solemn, ceremonial, and ritualistic service centering on sacrifice and silence.

But Jesus is showing them that a new relationship has come, in which they can have intimate contact with the bridegroom, and that it can only be expressed in joy and gladness and celebration.

The Scripture say, "In His presence there is fullness of joy."

We can have a new relationship with Jesus, one that changes constantly as it grows more intimate; one in which we must be sensitive to the fresh leading of the Holy Spirit, not encased in inflexible traditions.

One reason the Church is written off by so many today is that it is dead.

There is no joy, no celebration, and no life.

And in many cases, they are right.

In most churches, people sit with such long faces that you would think you were at a funeral.

And who likes to go to funerals? No wonder people do not come to many churches.

A lot of churches are dead.

Another reason why people write off the Church is because the church is not relevant.

It no longer speaks with biblical authority to the issues people are facing.

Many churches are answering questions no one is asking.

Today, people are crying out for a simple, straight-forward word from God about where they live.

The Church of Jesus needs to be both alive and relevant.

It needs to have a balance between zeal and truth.

And if we are open, God will give us that balance.

God desires to do a new thing in your life.

Are you open and flexible enough to receive it?

He desires to deepen your relationship, to bring you into new areas of ministry and service, to use you in a greater capacity.

But in order to do that, we must be willing to get out of the rut of the routine and to do things in a new way.

New wine must have new wineskins.

Are you willing to allow Jesus to upset the routine in your life in order to bring you to where He wants you to be?

He is far less concerned about those traditions we've set up than He is about meeting our human need.

Just has He reached forth to touch human need in each of these incidents we've studied today, so He will meet your need as well.

And as we let Him meet our needs, He will work through us to meet others' needs.

"Blessed are the flexible, for they shall not be broken."

Let me change it a bit: "Blessed are the flexible, for they are pliable in God's hands."

The Madness of Jesus

Mark 3:20-30

He is out of His mind! He's lost His senses! He's flipped out! I believe He's insane!

Would these be the reactions of our contemporary society to Jesus Christ, were He among us today?

Many people think that our world would welcome Jesus Christ into their midst; that Jesus would appear to them to be sensible and sane, the perfect balance of every human characteristic.

Human characteristics are fatally flawed as a result of the Fall.

Our perspective on things is warped, and I fear if Jesus came along today, our reaction to Him would be one of rejection.

But it was so in Jesus' day, even by the members of His own family.

If there were insane asylums in Jesus' day, He would have been committed.

The men would have been dispatched to place Him in a straight-jacket and take Him away.

And the ones who would do the committing would be His own family.

For that is precisely the opinion they express about Jesus in the first few verses of this passage we're studying today.

After all, what would your reaction be to a man who was flouting your traditions, preaching as if He has some special authority and revelation from God?

What would you think if He claimed that people were tormented by demons and then proceeded to cast them out?

And what if he were your relative, perhaps your son?

Well, that was precisely what Jesus was doing.

But instead of praising God because of the good He was doing, His own family though He was mad.

They thought He had taken leave of his senses, that He was a madman.

"And He came home, and the multitude gathered again, to such an extent that they could not even eat a meal. And when His own people heard of this, they went out to take custody of Him; for they were saying, 'He has lost His senses.'" (vv. 20-21)

After all, a little religion was a good thing.

But He had taken this too far, and He wasn't even following the traditions of the elders.

He had become a fanatic.

He was suffering from delusions of grandeur.

So, the only thing left to do was to go and bring Him back home, where He would be out of the public eye, and try to get Him some help.

This was their reasoning.

But to those who were used to seeing the limited vision of that day, this was not a wild conclusion.

Only those who were willing to see from God's point of view would come to see Christ as a man sent from God.

His family could not see. But there were many of His day, most notably the scribes and Pharisees, who could have seen, but chose not to.

So, His opposition from those who would not or could not see increased.

And in this passage, we have this opposition coming from two camps: from His own family, and from a delegation of scribes from Jerusalem.

Let's take a closer look at this passage today.

Imbedded in it are several important principles useful in our walk with the Lord.

Peril

Let's look firstly at the peril of a divided house.

"And the scribes who came down from Jerusalem were saying, 'He is possessed by Beelzebul,' and 'He casts out the demons by the ruler of the demons." And he called them to Himself and began speaking to them in parables, 'How can Satan cast out Satan? And if a kingdom is divided against itself, that kingdom cannot stand. And if a house is divided against itself, that house will not be able to stand. And if Satan has risen up against himself and is divided, he cannot stand, but he is finished!" (vv. 22-26)

Notice the scribes' accusation.

They had not come as objective observers.

They were a delegation sent from Jerusalem to accuse Jesus of error.

And their minds were already made up before they arrived.

You see, Jesus had been mounting a frontal assault on the kingdom of Satan.

Never before had one so aggressively undertaken to destroy Satan's work.

When Jesus had come upon demon possessed individuals, the demons could not keep quiet, but had to make themselves know.

And when they did, Jesus dealt with them.

He delivered those who were demon oppressed and cast the demons out.

For some reason, this upset those religious leaders who were witnessing these events.

And so, they leveled their simplistic and illogical charge at Him. "He is possessed by Beelzebul . . . He casts out the demons by the ruler of the demons."

Notice Jesus' reply.

It was so simple and so logical.

Basically all He said was that a house divided cannot stand.

He said that Satan would not oppose himself.

It was not logical.

How could the devil make any progress if his kingdom was always at odds with itself?

It simply could not survive under those conditions; and neither can any organization, business, family, or group.

This is a principle of life.

It is built into the order of the universe.

To oppose yourself is to fail at what you are trying to do.

Where there is opposition from within, all manner of problems arise.

It is like a cancer to the body.

It is a part of the body, but the cells are growing out of control and draining the life of the body, Cancer is the body at odds with itself.

And it can end in death if not corrected.

Many a malignancy exists in the organizations of men; and when they go unchecked, the demise of such organizations is sure.

Even in many churches do such cancers eat away at the unity of the Spirit.

And in some sad cases, they quench the Spirit's working in that body.

If we would enjoy the benefits of success in the Kingdom, we need to put unity and common vision on the list of our top priorities.

Do you know why so many churches fail in their mission?

It is because they are not going anywhere together.

Every member has his or her ideas of what ought to be done.

Everyone has their own agenda.

There is no common goal, no common vision.

Many times, they end up opposing each other.

They become a house divided.

I often wondered why, in my study of church growth, that although the growing churches which were studied differed in many respects, in every case there was one thing in common.

They all had strong pastoral leadership.

I believe I know why now.

It is a matter of vision.

Where the vision has been set, and where the people have caught the vision, the churches move forward, united in a common set of goals, working together.

Jesus had the vision for those who heard Him.

Those who were willing to be open to that vision and catch that vision, saw by faith and believed in Him as the Messiah.

These scribes never considered that the reason Jesus could cast out demons was that He was the Messiah, sent from God.

They were not open.

Their minds were already made up.

This man did not fit their theology.

How about you?

Is your mind already made up?

Are you quick to dismiss things based on the fact that they do not fit your ideas of how things ought to be?

We must catch the same vision and unite behind the person of Jesus Christ.

We must avoid getting hung up in peripheral issues and unite behind the goals that really count, lest we find ourselves to be a house divided.

If there is something that the Church at large needs today, it is to be consistent, united behind a common vision, moving together toward the same goal.

1 Corinthians 1:10 says,

"Now I exhort your, brethren, by the name of our Lord Jesus Christ, that you all agree, and there be no divisions among you, but you be made complete in the same mind and in the same judgment."

The peril of a divided house is that a house divided cannot stand.

Preeminence

Next, let's turn our attention to the preeminence of a victorious Savior.

"But no one can enter the strong man's house and plunder his property unless he first binds the strong man, and then he will plunder his house." (v.27)

Jesus has bound the strong man.

Notice the illustration Jesus uses.

The strong man is obviously Satan, so for Satan's house to be spoiled, he must first be bound.

And that is what was happening. Satan's house was being plundered by the Lord Jesus every time He cast out a demon.

So, the obvious conclusion was that Jesus was the stronger man who had bound the strong man of the house.

We see here the preeminence of a victorious Savior.

The power of the enemy had been broken.

Here is another principle of the Kingdom of God.

Jesus has broken the power of the enemy in our lives.

And we must see that fact and walk from that position.

But most Christians do not see that fact; much less walk from that position.

In fact, most of what is ours in Christ, we neither see nor walk in.

It all begins with understanding that Jesus is the victorious One.

He has bound the strong man.

Satan is a defected foe at the hands of Jesus Christ.

The hoards of hell cringe at the very mention of His name.

The enemy cowers as a defected foe at the mighty hand of Jesus.

And we, by faith, can enter into that victory, but we must begin to see ourselves as part of the victorious army of God.

And by faith, we must begin to exercise the diving prerogative we have to walk in that victory won for us by Christ himself.

The preeminence of victorious Savior means that all the promises of God are a resounding "yes" to us.

Presumption

Finally, let's turn our attention to the presumption of a blasphemous attitude.

"Truly I say to you, all sins shall be forgiven the sons of men, and whatever blasphemies they utter; but whoever blasphemes against the Holy Spirit never has forgiveness, but is guilty of an eternal sin' – because they were saying, 'He has an unclean spirit." (vv. 28-30)

Notice what the scribes had done.

They had attributed the work of God to Satan.

They had called the work of the Spirit of God the work of the devil.

Their presumptuous and blasphemous attitude was putting their souls in eternal peril.

Many today do this same thing.

And it is usually the same kind of people who do it – religious people.

When the Lord begins a work in the lives of people and they cannot fit it into their theology, they are quick to say it is of the devil.

But this is exactly what the scribes did, and it is very dangerous.

We must be extremely careful before we attribute what may be the work of God to the devil.

You see, your attitude makes all the difference.

Jesus points out here that this attitude which the scribes exhibited is the same attitude which resides in those who commit the unpardonable sin.

It is the attitude of rejecting the Spirit's work and witness.

Many people have had long discussions as they try to determine just what is the unpardonable sin.

I believe we receive tremendous insight from the lips of Jesus here.

It seems that the unpardonable sin is a continued, willful rejection of the Spirit's witness of Jesus.

The Spirit has been given to bear witness of Jesus.

He comes to you to convict you of the sin in your life, and to convince you that Jesus is the way of salvation.

When you harden your heart against that witness and say no, you are in essence calling the Spirit a liar.

When a person continually does that, there can be no forgiveness, for they will die in their sin and be forever lost in eternity.

The forgiveness of Christ is infinite.

There is no sin outside the bounds of His redemptive work.

All sins, even what we consider to be the most horrible, can be and are forgiven by Christ.

But this attitude of rejecting the Spirit's witness to Christ can never be forgiven because it keeps one from coming to Christ.

If you do not come to Christ, you place yourself outside the boundary of His redemptive work.

You can never be forgiven because you have rejected Christ.

It begins as an attitude of self-reliance, self-centeredness.

It is saying no to the Spirit's appeal and pleading in our lives.

Now, we as Christians also sin against the Holy Spirit.

Our sin as Christians is not the unpardonable sin of rejecting Jesus, but it is sin nonetheless.

When we hear the voice of God speaking to us from whatever source, and do not respond, we are quenching the Spirit.

When we choose self over the Holy Spirit's will that He has revealed to us, we grieve the Spirit.

Now you may say, "I would never do that. If I heard the voice of the Spirit speaking to me, I would obey Him. But I'm not going to do something because man says it."

Well, you are never going to hear what the Lord says to you if you have that attitude.

I'm sure the scribes were willing to hear God if He were to speak to them as He spoke to Moses.

But they were not willing to hear a man, Jesus.

If you would hear the Spirit speak, you will have to be open to hear Him speak through others, because that is how God speaks to us many times.

For some reason, God has chosen to use people to communicate His message.

Now, that is not to say that it does not confirm His Word to your heart inwardly; He certainly does.

The inward witness of the Spirit and the objective witness of the written word all confirm words of guidance received from others.

But the Spirit delights to you through those around you.

It is a good thing to have to hear God speak through others.

This works the character of Christ into our spirit.

You see, you must become humble in order to receive from others.

Your arrogant self-reliance must go.

There is an acknowledgement of your dependence on the rest of the body of Christ.

All of these things are things we need as believers.

Your attitude makes all the difference.

The unpardonable sin is a blasphemous attitude of rejecting the Spirit's witness to Christ.

Taken in its fullest sense, it is the unpardonable sin.

We must be careful as Christians, however, not to allow any attitudes which are cousins to this blasphemous attitude to enter our lives.

You see, to go our own way is to quench and grieve the Holy Spirit.

It is to sin against Him.

We must have the attitude that all we are and all we have is the Lord's.

We must have the attitude of surrender; the attitude which causes us to abandon our lives into the hands of Jesus.

You see, when we hold anything to ourselves, we are sinning against the lordship of Christ.

If He is not Lord of all, He is not Lord at all.

Let me ask you: is there any area of your life you are not holding onto apart from God?

Has the Spirit of God told you what you need to do in that area and you have not done it?

Let me say something rather direct to you: You are living in willful disobedience to the Lord.

That may sound rather harsh, but it really isn't.

We need to hear and obey.

Some of you have been struggling with your own selfish desires for too long.

You have been unwilling to give up unconditionally to the Lord.

You have certain pet areas in your life you still cling to.

You have certain opinions in which you think you are right and you will not yield.

You are forever fighting for your rights, not knowing that you must lay down your rights to have any.

Perhaps today you have seen the need to be a uniting factor in the local body here.

You see you have been anything but positive and supportive, and you need to make that right.

A house divided cannot stand.

Catch the vision.

Commit yourself to it.

Decide that you will walk hand in hand with the other brothers and sisters here to see God's work accomplished in this place.

Perhaps you see in your life some of the cynical attitude the scribes held.

Perhaps you see that you have been guilty, not of blasphemy of the Holy Spirit, but of quenching and grieving the Spirit.

If today you have come to understand that because of your unwillingness to yield to Him, you have been missing out on the abundant life, then yield to Him today.

Don't let another moment go by without drawing close to the Lord.

Ask Him to give you faith-filled attitudes instead of cynical ones.

As you draw near to God, He will draw near to you.

Kingdom Growth

Note: Read Mark 4:1-20

Mark 4:21-29

When for some reason a child does not develop properly, we all grieve over that sad situation. Babies are wonderful. When they come into this world, they are small and cute, cranky but cuddly.

They are indeed wonderful, and we thank God for them. But we also thank God that they grow up. A perpetual baby would be a tragic thing indeed. They, by God's grace, grow physically and emotionally, mentally, and spiritually. We all do.

As a matter of fact, if we are functioning properly, we should grow throughout out lives in one way or another. When we quit growing physically, we continue to grow emotionally, mentally, and hopefully, spiritually.

Stunted growth in a person is a tragedy. But stunted growth in the Kingdom of God is also a tragedy. God has created His Kingdom to grow. The Kingdom of God should be ever-expanding, one in which we are actively involved. Kingdom growth is something in which every Christian ought to be involved.

Jesus has given the Great Commission to all of us. And with the commission goes the power to see it accomplished.

Our text today shares with us a parable about Kingdom growth. In it, we see the secret of that growth. And perhaps as we study it, we can understand how we can more effectively assist in that growth.

Of all the parables, this one appears only in Mark. It is not like what some would mistake for its counterpart in Matthew, that is, the parable of the wheat and the tares. Some would have these two parables be variations of the same parable because in each, the farmer is said to plant the seed and go to sleep.

In each, the harvest comes when the seed has become ripe. There are similarities. But there are differences as well.

There is a different message in each of these parables. In the first, the emphasis is placed on the work of the enemy in sowing the tares, or darnell (a wheat look-alike), and in the action of the Lord in separating them for reward and judgment in His second coming.

But in the parable which we shall look today, the emphasis is placed on the secret growth of the seed because of the life contained within. These parables are distinct.

Here again, the seed is the Word of God. God's Word is the agent of growth in the Kingdom. We looked, in a previous reading beginning with Chapter 4, at the parable of the sower and the soils.

As the seed, which is the Word of God, is received into the good soil, it produces fruit. The Kingdom will grow as the seed is planted and as the seed matures. The seed has life in itself, and we must sow that seed in order to see the Kingdom grow.

We shall examine four aspects of Kingdom growth suggested to us by our text: First, the deliberate planting of the seed; second, the secret destiny of the seed; third, the progressive unfolding of the seed; and fourth, the proper harvesting of the seed.

Deliberate Planting

He also said, "This is what the kingdom of God is like. A man scatters seed on the ground" (v. 26).

The first truth which reveals itself to us is an obvious truth, but it needs emphasis. The seed must first be planted. Some today assume the seed of the Word of God is already planted there in people. But this is a false assumption to make. In order for anything at all to happen in a person's life, there must be the deliberate planting of the seed in the soil.

We have already seen that the type of soil on which the seed falls does have a direct effect on the result of the planting. The seed sown on hard ground by the wayside gets stolen by the devil.

The seed that is sown on shallow ground without much depth is starved for lack of root.

The seed sown on thorny ground is choked by the cares of the world, the deceitfulness or riches, and the desire for other things.

And the seed sown on good, prepared and cultivated ground produces fruit, thirty, sixty, and a hundredfold.

What we are looking at here is seed sown on good ground. The kind of soil here has been prepared by the Holy Spirit and is ready to receive the seed. But the seed must first be sown by someone.

Somehow, the seed must fall upon this earth to begin to have any effect at all.

How do we sow the seed? As Christians, we desire to see people come into the same vital, living relationship with Jesus that we personally have with the Lord Jesus Christ.

That should be the desire of every Christian. If you know and love Jesus Christ, you should desire for others to know and love Him also. Jesus has come into your life. He has made a radical change in you. You have been the recipient of His love and grace.

His mercy has been showered upon you. Once you were lost in your sins, and without hope. Once you were blind, but Jesus came along. Now, you are forgiven. Now you have hope. Now you can see. He has healed your hurts. He has given you new life. Once you were desperate and confused. Now you have a purpose for living. All of this has been accomplished by Jesus Christ.

And you desire for others to know Him. But in order for them to come to know Him, the seed must be sown in their hearts.

We sow the seed by sharing Jesus. And the ways in which this can be done are numerous. In fact, we have probably not even scratched the surface in thinking of the many ways in which we can share the life of Jesus with others.

And so, we desire to know every way of sowing seed. If there is a new way, we desire to know it so others can come to know Jesus Christ.

Now, the message of the Word of God never changes. It is the same old message the apostles preached. It is the simple gospel message of a sweet salvation bought for us by the sacrifice of our Savior.

And it is true that somehow the simple message of the saving Gospel must be told to the one we are trying to win. But we all know that what takes the most thought is how we can create a situation in which we can share the Lord in such a way that the person will be open to what we say.

In this regard, the opportunities are vast. Our problem is that we do not think creatively enough in today's world.

Sometimes our problem is that we are too embarrassed. We are afraid we might make a fool out of ourselves. But let me ask you: what is more important, your ego or the salvation of some dear lost soul?

I heard of one preacher who used to get on elevators. And as the door closed, he would say to the man beside him, "Which way is the last trip you're ever going to take, is it up or down?"

Well, that might not be your style, but it would sure get you on the topic. The point is that if we are willing to break out of our mold and try some new things, we might be surprised at the ideas the Lord would give us. Prayerfully consider creative ways you can share with your friends, neighbors, associates, and family.

Let those ideas be born in prayer. But let them be born to insure Kingdom growth.

We must deliberately plant the seed if we would ever see a harvest. There must be a determined effort to share with people the simple story of saving grace. And you must be the one to share it. You may be the only Gospel preacher they ever hear.

Your life may be the only truly Christian witness they ever see. Have you shared the Word with them? Have you planted the seed in their hearts? Have you told them of what Jesus has done for you and what He can do for them? Plant the seed. Plant it however you will, but plant it in their hearts.

Secret Destiny

Night and day, whether he sleeps or gets up, the seed sprouts and grows, through he does not know how. All by itself the soil produces grain-- (vv. 27-28a)

Notice the sower's limited power. There is only so much that the sower can do. If he has done his job in cultivation and preparation of the land, then after he has sown the seed he must let it alone.

We must cultivate and prepare the lives of those in whose heart we would sow the seed. There is much work in this initial stage. We must be friends to those without the Gospel of Christ. We must open our hearts and our homes to them.

This takes time and much effort. But it is all part of that cultivation process by which we earn the right to share the good news with them.

Just as a farmer works diligently to break up the ground in his field, to till the soil, to use fertilizers, and engage in other processes to enrich the soil and rid it of weeds and insects, so we must use every means available to us to cultivate the heart of that person we would see receive Jesus.

But then we must sow the seed and let it alone. This is what the farmer does in our text.

Our text says that he rises and sleeps night and day. In other words, he goes on living his life as usual, day after day. He does not see the seed under the soil. He only hopes everything is going well. He can't dig it up to see how it is doing. He can't tell how much of it is going to come up until he sees the stalk break through the ground.

Even then, he can't tell how much of it will produce. He has little knowledge of the weather and other factors which he can't predict. He must trust in the life of the seed. He has done what he can do.

But the message is that the seed does grow. The point that the Lord is trying to make is that because of the life contained in the seed, it grows.

The farmer does not understand how that really works, but he knows that it does work. That is why he plants.

We do not have to understand God's work either. We know certain things work and we take full advantage of them. We do not have to understand how electricity works to turn on the lights.

As we sow the seed, there are processes at work to bring forth the germination of that seed. As we share the Gospel message and plant it in the hearts of lost people, God will see to it that the word accomplishes the purpose for which He has ordained it.

Now, this gives us hope for many. In our evangelistic efforts, we may not see immediate success. But that is not a reason for discouragement. The seed sown may be in the progress of germination under the soil, and we not even know it.

The word sown in the heart may be having its effect, even when we can't see it.

Many times, we are guilty of giving up too soon on the seed because we can't see it. But according to this parable, the Lord may have everything on schedule.

There is a secret destiny of the seed because of the life contained in it. The Word of God is a living thing. It is not merely information. It is not simply historical fact. The Word of God has a life of its own. It is the life of the breath of God.

Progressive Unfolding

All by itself the soil produces grain—first the stalk, then the head, then the full kernel in the head (v. 28).

The progress of the seed is through several stages. In the growth of the seed, it does not go from a grain to the full ear of corn. It does not pass from the planting stage to the harvesting stage overnight.

It must pass through several growth stages first. These growth stages are spoken of here as the blade, the head, and the mature grain in the head.

What is true of an ear of corn is true of people as well. People must pass through stages of preparation. When the seed of the Word of God is dropped into the hearts of those to whom we are witnessing, the process begins.

If the heart is "good ground" then the Word may come to harvest. But it must be watered by the continued efforts of those who care.

It must withstand the elements that can come against it by Satan. Again, as it passes through the various stages of growth, it may come to that place where it is ready for harvest.

God is at work to bring forth the seed to full harvest. Some of us have the privilege to sow that seed. By sharing the Word, others of us have the privilege to water that seed. We do not have the power to cause the seed to grow.

There is a progressive unfolding of that seed by God's grace. Salvation is of God. We are merely His instruments.

Paul said, in First Corinthians 3:6-7, "I planted, Apollos watered, but God was causing the growth. So then neither the one who plants nor the one who waters is anything, but God who causes the growth."

God will use the seed we plant and the care in watering we provide to cause that seed to progressively come to maturity. You can count on it. But we must be faithful in planting and water. If we are, we will be privileged to participate in the harvesting.

Proper Harvesting

As soon as the grain is ripe, he puts the sickle to it, because the harvest has come (v. 29).

Only as the seed becomes ripe can it be harvested. Verse 29 gives us the pattern for harvest. When the seed becomes ripe, then it is ready for harvest.

No farmer would think of pulling up a young plant as soon as it broke through the ground. There would be no point.

It would do the farmer no good. That would be financial suicide for the farmer. There is nothing to be harvested.

The same is true in regard to souls. When we do not allow the processes of God to work, we get no real results that last. All we can do is sow the seed, be faithful to water that seed, and allow God to do His work.

All of us are different. We all must go through different stages of preparation before harvest. So many times we who sow the seed are eager to harvest that crop before it is ripe. We must be patient and allow God to deal with that individual. When the time comes, we will find the field ripe.

Now, this does not discourage evangelism. You may say that to have this kind of mentality throws a wet blanket on our efforts to see people come to Christ.

Some could easily say that there is no use to try to get people saved now — that perhaps they are not yet ready for harvest. But while some may use this as an excuse, there is no excuse there.

Jesus said that the fields were white unto harvest. There are always those who are ready to be harvested. As we continually and conscientiously sow seed, there will always be some who are fully mature, fully ripe, and ready to be harvested.

We cannot use the maturing process of the seed as an excuse for not winning people to Jesus. If we do, our real problem is that we have no heart for souls.

Rather than discouraging immediate evangelistic effort, it encourages it. You see, the harvest in which we are involved is not a seasonal thing.

There is fruit getting ripe every day in God's field. Somewhere, someone is being prepared for the harvest each moment. The process may have gone on for months, even years. But at this very moment they are responding to the Lord.

Some harvester somewhere is reaping the reward of another's labor.

So it is our place to be out in the field, ready to harvest those who are becoming ripe. We must learn to tell when that is. So as a good husbandman, we can put in the sickle and come forth bringing our sheaves with us.

As we sow the seed, the seed will grow. The exhortation of God to us is to keep showing wherever you go, whatever you do.

Keep on scattering seeds. When you are in the supermarket, plant a seed. When you are in the office, plant a seed.

When you are talking with your neighbor across the fence, plant a seed. As you do, God will begin to cause those seeds to germinate. He will give a great increase. Let's keep on sowing.

God is using our efforts as we are faithful to plant those seeds and give ourselves to the work. So cultivate that soil, plant that seed, water it and stand back and watch God work.

Harvest time is near.

A:\SERMON.762
Revised, 5-10-05

"SURVIVING STORMS"

TEXT: MARK 4:35-41

IN JANUARY OF 1975

LATE ONE AFTERNOON THE TELEPHONE RANG IN OUR HOME in Burney Indiana, at the parsonage of the first church I served.

It was NEWS THAT WE CERTAINLY DIDN'T WANT TO HEAR.

MY ONLY BROTHER, MIKE, WHO WAS THEN AGE 20, HAD BEEN INSTANTLY KILLED IN AN AUTO WRECK.

THE TRUTH SET IN AND WE CRIED TOGETHER FOR A WHILE, THEN WE BOOKED A FLIGHT THAT SAME NIGHT AND CAME HOME TO PREPARE FOR HIS FUNERAL.

MIKE HAD ENJOYED LIFE SO MUCH, BUT NOW HE WAS GONE.

18 YEARS LATER, MY FATHER HAD A HEART ATTACK THAT PROVED FATAL WITH THE OTHER COMPLICATIONS HE CONTRACTED IN THE HOSPITAL, SUCH AS A STAFF INFECTION, AND HE COULDN'T OVERCOME.

THEN EARLY ON THE MORNING OF JUNE 1, 1996, THE TELEPHONE RANG, AND WE LEARNED THAT a near cousin, THE YOUNG MAN WE PRACTICALLY RAISED AS OUR OWN SON, HAD BEEN KILLED IN A WRECK IN COLUMBIA, SC.

This year, we've lost 9 family members, cousins, etc.

AS YOUR PASTOR, GOD HAS EQUIPPED ME WITH SOME PERSONAL STORMS TO HELP PREPARE ME TO SERVE YOU.

I DON'T KNOW WHAT STORM YOU'RE FACING OR WILL FACE IN YOUR LIFE IN THE FUTURE, BUT I DO KNOW THERE ARE SOME VERY INSTRUCTIVE PRINCIPLES IN MARK 4:35-41, THAT IF APPLIED WITH THE POWER OF GOD, WILL ENABLE YOU TO SURVIVE WHATEVER STORMS YOU ENCOUNTER IN LIFE.

READ MARK 4:35-41

Prayer:

FATHER, WE BOW BEFORE YOU WITH HUMBLED HEARTS SEEKING TO EXPERIENCE THE WONDER AND MAJESTY OF YOUR AMAZING GRACE. AS WE PARTICIPATE IN YOUR GRAND SCHEME WITHIN OUR LIVES, MAY OUR LIVES CONTINUE TO SING YOUR PRAISES AS WE WORK TOGETHER HERE IN OUR CHURCH AND COMMUNITY.

FATHER, WE PRAISE YOU FOR REVEALING YOURSELF IN THE WRITTEN WORD AS YOU DECLARE YOUR LOVE FOR A LOST AND SINFUL WORLD.

FORGIVE US WHEN WE'RE UNGRATEFUL FOR ALL THAT YOU DO AND ALL YOU GIVE TO US; FOR WE CONFESS OUR LACK OF THANKFULNESS TO YOU.

OUR PRAYER Today, AS WE STUDY FROM THE GOSPEL OF MARK, IS THAT WE WOULD STRIVE FOR TOTAL COMMITMENT TO YOU AS WE COMMIT TO YOUR PLANS FOR OUR LIVES. REMIND US FOR THE NEED OF PERSONAL COMMITMENT, AS WE PRAY TO YOU IN THE NAME OF JESUS CHRIST, OUR LORD AND SAVIOR. AMEN.

WHAT ARE SOME WAYS WE CAN SURVIVE THE STORMS OF LIFE?

I.   FIRST, BE INFORMED ABOUT STORMS.

JESUS WAS PHYSICALLY AND EMOTIONALLY EXHAUSTED FROM AN INTENSIVE DAY OF TEACHING.

HE FELL ASLEEP IN THE BOAT ON A CALM LAKE WHILE HIS DISCIPLES HEADED TO THE OTHER SHORE.

THEN THE STORM BEGAN.

THERE ARE TWO KEY THINGS YOU NEED TO KNOW ABOUT STORMS.

FIRST, STORMS COME UNEXPECTEDLY AS WE READ IN VERSES 35 AND 36.

THE SEA OF GALILEE IS 620 FEET BELOW SEA LEVEL AND IS SURROUNDED BY MOUNTAINS WITH DEEP VALLEYS.

THE VALLEYS SERVE AS GIGANTIC FUNNELS TO FOCUS THE WHIRLING WINDS DOWN UPON THE SEA.

A SEVERE STORM CAN ARISE WITHOUT NOTICE WITH TERRIFYING RESULTS.

IN THE SAME WAY, STORMS OFTEN COME INTO OUR LIVES WITHOUT ANY WARNING WHATEVER.

WHEN EVERYTHING SEEMS TO BE GOING GOOD AND WE THINK WE CAN SIT BACK AND ENJOY LIFE, OUT OF NOWHERE A STORM OF DEVASTATING PROPORTION MAY TAKE US BY SURPRISE, TURNING OUR LIFE UPSIDE DOWN.

SECOND, STORMS COME WITH LOTS OF FURY.

IT WASN'T JUST A LITTLE ROUGHNESS OUT THERE ON THE SEA OF GALILEE.

IT WAS AN INCREDIBLE SQUALL THAT THREATENED TO SINK THE BOAT.

THE STORMS THAT COME SO SUDDENLY AND THREATEN TO SINK US MAY BE IN THE WORD "CANCER".

OR IT MAY BE IN THE WORD "SUDDEN DEATH" OF A LOVED ONE AS MANY OF US HAVE EXPERIENCED SEVERAL TIMES.

ANY NUMBER OF THINGS CAN LEAVE US WONDERING HOW WE WILL EVER SURVIVE THE STORM.

SO, FROM THE BIBLE, WE LEARN THAT STORMS COME UNEXPECTEDLY AND WITH LOTS OF FURY.

THE KEY TO SURVIVAL IS TO BE PREPARED.

IT'S VERY DIFFICULT TO GET PREPARED DURING THE STORM.
SO THERE NEEDS TO BE PRIOR PREPARATION.

II.   THAT BRINGS US TO THE SECOND MAJOR POINT
        BEING PREPARED FOR STORMS.

LOOK AT VERSES 38-41 AS WE STUDY THEM TOGETHER.

PREPARATION IS A CONTINUOUS PROCESS.

THE MORE WE'RE PREPARED, THE BETTER WE'LL BE ABLE TO SURVIVE THE STORMS OF LIFE.

PREPARATION COMES THROUGH KNOWING CERTAIN TRUTHS THAT ARE REVEALED TO US IN THE BIBLE.

WE NEED TO KNOW THOSE TRUTHS AND LET THEM BECOME CONVICTIONS THAT GRIP US AS THEY CHANGE AND SHAPE OUR LIVES.

I WANT TO GIVE YOU 7 WAYS WE CAN BE PREPARED FOR STORMS.

1.   FIRST, WE NEED TO KNOW THAT JESUS CARES.

IN VERSE 38, WE LEARN THAT THE STORM DIDN'T WAKE JESUS UP.

THE CRIES OF THE MEN WOKE HIM UP.

THEIR QUESTION WAS, "DON'T YOU CARE?

WE'RE OFTEN TEMPTED TO ASK GOD THE SAME QUESTION.

SOMETIMES IT APPEARS THAT GOD IS EITHER INDIFFERENT TO THE STORMS THAT HIT US, OR HE IS IGNORANT OF WHAT WE'RE GOING THROUGH.

EVEN WHEN IT SEEMS TO US THAT GOD MAY BE INDIFFERENT OR THAT HE DOESN'T CARE, WE CAN KNOW AND TRUST THE TRUTH OF FIRST PETER 5:7 WHERE THE BIBLE SAYS "CAST ALL YOUR ANXIETY ON HIM BECAUSE HE CARES FOR YOU."

JESUS CARES!

HE LOVED AND CARED SO MUCH FOR US THAT HE DIED ON THE CROSS.

WE NEED THE CONVICTION WITHIN OUR HEARTS THAT HE CARES DEEPLY FOR US AND IS INTENSELY COMPASSIONATE ABOUT EVERYTHING THAT AFFECTS US, OR WILL EVER AFFECT OUR LIVES.

2.   SECOND, WE NEED TO KNOW THAT JESUS ISN'T SURPRISED BY OUR STORMS OF LIFE.

LOOK AT VERSE 39.

JESUS WASN'T SURPRISED BY THE STORM ON THE SEA OF GALILEE.

HE SIMPLY GOT UP AND SPOKE TO THE WAVES.

IN FACT, JESUS KNEW THE STORM WAS COMING FOR HIS DISCIPLES.

IT WAS PART OF THAT DAY'S CURRICULUM.

GOD IS ALWAYS AWARE OF EVERYTHING THAT'S GOING TO HAPPEN TO YOU.

PSALM 139 MAKES IT VERY CLEAR THAT GOD KNOWS ALL THE EVENTS OF OUR LIVES.
THE BIBLE SAYS THAT "BEFORE A WORD IS ON MY TONGUE...GOD KNOWS IT COMPLETELY (PSALM 139:4).

HE'S NOT SHOCKED OR SURPRISED AT ALL AT WHAT HAPPENS TO US.

IT'S PART OF HIS PLAN AND PURPOSE FOR OUR LIVES.

WE NEED TO BE CONVINCED THAT GOD HAS THE STORMS OF OUR LIVES UNDER HIS CONTROL.

3.   THIRD, WE NEED TO KNOW THAT JESUS WILL ACT UPON THE STORMS.

IN THE CASE OF THE DISCIPLES, JESUS ACTED IMMEDIATELY.

"HE GOT UP, REBUKED THE WIND, AND SAID TO THE WAVES, "QUIET! BE STILL!

THEN THE WIND DIED DOWN AND THE SEA WAS COMPLETELY CALM.

HE BROUGHT IMMEDIATE CALM TO THEIR LIVES.

HE'S STILL ABLE TO ACT THAT WAY FOR US, AND SOMETIMES HE DOES---BUT NOT ALWAYS.

IN FACT, MORE OFTEN JESUS DOESN'T WORK IMMEDIATELY IN THE STORMS OF OUR LIVES.

WE DON'T KNOW WHEN OR HOW GOD'S GOING TO ACT.

WE CAN'T DICTATE GOD'S TIMETABLE, BUT WE CAN BE ASSURED THAT GOD WILL ACT IN HIS PERFECT WAY IN HIS PERFECT TIMING.

WE ALWAYS WANT GOD TO ACT ON OUR TIMETABLE.

WE WANT TO TELL GOD, "IF YOU WOULD JUST DO THIS MY WAY, EVERYTHING WILL BE FINE.

BUT DEEP INSIDE, WE KNOW THAT GOD'S WAYS ARE HIGHER THAN OUR WAYS.

4.   IN THE MEANTIME, WE NEED TO KNOW THAT JESUS IS WITH US.

IN THE STORM ON THE SEA OF GALILEE, JESUS NEVER LEFT HIS DISCIPLES.

HE WAS RIGHT THERE IN THE BOAT WITH THEM.

WE NEED TO BE AWARE OF HIS PRESENCE WITH US SO WE CAN EXPERIENCE HIS PEACE, NO MATTER WHAT PARTICULAR STORM WE'RE GOING THROUGH.

ISAIAH 43:2 SAYS, "WHEN YOU PASS THROUGH THE WATERS; I WILL BE WITH YOU...

THAT MEANS THAT WHATEVER THE TRIALS WE GO THROUGH, GOD IS WITH US AND HE WILL GO THROUGH THEM WITH US.

IT'S SAFER TO BE IN THE MIDDLE OF THE STORM WITH GOD'S PRESENCE THAN TO HAVE NO STORM AND BE WITHOUT GOD.

WHAT A GREAT COMFORT IT IS TO KNOW THAT GOD WILL NEVER LEAVE US OR FORSAKE US, AND HE WILL TAKE US SAFELY THROUGH THE STORM.

5.   FIFTH, JESUS MADE IT VERY CLEAR TO HIS DISCIPLES WHERE THEY WERE GOING.

THEY WERE GOING TO THE OTHER SIDE OF THE LAKE.

HE DIDN'T PROMISE THEM AN EASY TRIP.

HE DID, HOWEVER, GUARANTEE THEY WOULD ARRIVE AT THEIR DESTINATION.

BY FAITH THEY SHOULD HAVE CLAIMED THAT, AND SO SHOULD WE.

IF WE CLAIM HIM AS OUR PERSONAL SAVIOR, OUR FAITH IN HIM TEACHES US THAT JESUS IS TAKING US SAFELY TO THE OTHER SIDE, TO HEAVEN, TO SPEND ETERNITY WITH HIM.

NOTHING CAN STOP THAT.

THE BIBLE SAYS IN JOB 42:2 "I KNOW THAT YOU CAN DO ALL THINGS; NO PLAN OF YOURS CAN BE THWARTED.

AND IN PHILIPPIANS 1:6, THE BIBLE AFFIRMS, "...HE WHO BEGAN A GOOD WORK IN YOU WILL CARRY IT ON TO COMPLETION UNTIL THE DAY OF CHRIST JESUS.

STORMS ARE A PART OF THE PROCESS OF OUR SPIRITUAL GROWTH.

IN OUR STORY IN MARK, JESUS WAS GOING TO THE OTHER SIDE AND THE DISCIPLES WERE GOING WITH HIM.

YOU CAN COUNT ON TWO THINGS:
    THE BOAT WON'T SINK!
    THE STORMS OF LIFE WON'T LAST FOREVER.

6.   SIXTH, WE NEED TO KNOW THAT JESUS CHRIST IS SOVEREIGN.

THE DISCIPLES HAD ALREADY SEEN THAT JESUS WAS THE MASTER OF EVERY SITUATION.

NOW THEIR KNOWLEDGE WAS PUT TO THE TEST.

CAN GOD HANDLE YOUR SITUATION THAT YOU'RE IN RIGHT NOW?

YOU BET HE CAN!

THERE'S NOTHING TOO DIFFICULT FOR GOD.

7.   SEVENTH, WE NEED TO KNOW OUR GREATEST NEED.

OUR BIGGEST PROBLEM ISN'T THE STORMS THAT COME INTO OUR LIVES, IT'S OUR UNBELIEF.

THE ONLY THING JESUS EVER REBUKED THE DISCIPLES FOR WAS THEIR LACK OF FAITH.

OUR GREATEST PROBLEMS COME FROM WITHIN US, BECAUSE WE DON'T HAVE THAT DEEP SOLID CONVICTION THAT GOD CARES.

WE LACK FAITH NOT ONLY TO BELIEVE THAT GOD CARES, BUT WE LACK FAITH TO BELIEVE THAT GOD WILL ACT FOR US IN OUR PARTICULAR SITUATIONS.

THE DISCIPLES HAD SEEN JESUS PERFORM MIRACLES.

BUT WHEN IT CAME RIGHT DOWN TO IT, THEY STILL HAD NO FAITH THAT HE COULD WORK IN THEIR SITUATION.

HEBREWS SAYS, "WITHOUT FAITH IT IS IMPOSSIBLE TO PLEASE GOD."

III.   VERSE 41 TEACHES US TO BE TRANSFORMED BY
         THE STORM.

THE DISCIPLES WERE LITERALLY TERRIFIED.

GOING THROUGH THE STORM AND SURVIVING IT HAD A POWERFUL IMPACT UPON THEIR LIVES.

ONE THING ABOUT STORMS WE CAN BE SURE OF: STORMS NEVER LEAVE US WHERE THEY FIND US.

SOME PEOPLE GO THROUGH STORMS AND COME OUT THE OTHER SIDE BITTER AND ANGRY WITH GOD, AND NEGATIVE ABOUT LIFE.

SOME PEOPLE, WHO ARE WEAK IN THEIR FAITH, BREAK DOWN WHEN A STORM COMES.

THEY LOSE CONTROL AND THEY LOSE HOPE.

THEY FALL APART AND ARE TOTALLY DEVASTATED.

THEN THERE ARE OTHERS WHO ARE SO STRONG WILLED, THEY BECOME HARDENED AND ANGRY WITH GOD AND WITH OTHER PEOPLE, AND THEY BECOME UNTOUCHABLE.

THEN THERE ARE THOSE WHO GO THROUGH THE STORM AND DON'T BREAK DOWN.

THEY GO TO A NEW DIMENSION OF THEIR SPIRITUAL LIFE.

THEY COME THROUGH THE STORM WITH THEIR FAITH DEEPENED AND THEIR PRIORITIES REARRANGED.

THEY BECOME MORE OF THE PERSON CHRIST WOULD HAVE THEM TO BE.

THEY BECOME MORE PEACEFUL AND MORE SURE OF GOD'S POWER IN THEIR LIVES.

THEY BECOME MORE USEFUL SERVANTS OF GOD.

STORMS IN YOUR LIFE WILL DO ONE OF TWO THINGS:
        DEFORM YOU
        OR TRANSFORM YOU.

THE DIFFERENCE WILL BE YOUR FAITH AND YOUR COOPERATION WITH GOD.

SOME OF YOU WHO ARE HERE Today SEEM TO HAVE MORE THAN YOUR SHARE OF STORMS.

I DON'T HAVE AN EASY ANSWER TO WHY YOU HAVE THOSE DIFFICULT STORMS!

WHAT HAPPENS WHEN A STORM TAKES PLACE IN YOUR LIFE WILL BE DETERMINE BY HOW YOU'RE PREPARED.

THE WAY TO GET PREPARED IS TO KNOW THESE TRUTHS THAT I'VE SHARED WITH YOU THIS MORNING AND ALLOW THEM TO BECOME SETTLED CONVICTIONS IN YOUR LIFE.

THEN WHATEVER STORM COMES YOUR WAY, YOU'LL BE TRANSFORMED.

YOU'LL BECOME MORE LIKE CHRIST AND COOPERATE WITH GOD AS STORMS COME INTO YOUR LIFE.

BE INFORMED ABOUT STORMS.

BE PREPARED.

AND BE TRANSFORMED BY GOD'S AMAZING GRACE!

SURVIVING STORMS
Mark 4:35-41

Introduction: Some of my personal storms

What are some ways we can survive the storms of life?

II.   Be informed about storms
      1.   Storms come unexpectedly
      2.   Storms come with lots of fury

II.   Seven ways to be prepared for storms
      3.   Know that Jesus cares
      4.   Know that Jesus isn't surprised by our storms
      5.   Know that Jesus will act upon our storms
      6.   Know that Jesus is with us
      7.   Know that Jesus knows where we're going
      8.   Know that Jesus Christ is sovereign
      9.   Know our greatest need

III.   Be transformed by storms by God's Amazing Grace

SERMON.797
SEE # 653 & BURNEY SERMON

WHAT DO YOU WANT WITH ME, JESUS?

TEXT: MARK 5:1-20

DEAR HEAVENLY FATHER, WE THANK YOU FOR YOUR POWER OVER ALL THE EVENTS AND CIRCUMSTANCES IN OUR LIVES. WE ALSO THANK YOU FOR ALL THE Heavenly spiritual FORCES WHICH INFLUENCE US. WE KNOW

THAT YOU ARE ABLE TO help us with all of our circumstances. WE PRAISE YOU TODAY FOR ALLOWING US TO WORSHIP HERE IN THIS BEAUTIFUL SANCTUARY, AND WE PRAY THAT EVERYONE HERE This afternoon WILL HAVE OPEN MINDS TO THE MESSAGE YOU WOULD HAVE for US TO HERE IN THIS BIBLE PASSAGE. IN JESUS NAME WE PRAY. AMEN.

THIS scripture passage we have read TEACHES US OF THE GREAT THINGS JESUS CAN DO.

THE SETTING IS THE GREEK DECAPOLIS--A CENTER OF 10 HELLENISTIC GREEK CITIES THAT JESUS VISITED DURING HIS EARTHLY MINISTRY.

HERE, JESUS IS VISITING THE CITY OF GARDARA, AFTER HE HAS CROSSED OVER INTO THE REGION EAST OF THE JORDAN RIVER.

JESUS IS AT THE END OF A VERY demanding DAY OF TEACHING, MINISTERING, AND HEALING.

HE WAS PHYSICALLY WORN OUT AFTER HE CALMED THE STORM ON THE SEA OF GALILEE.

NOW, HE'S HAD A CHANCE TO GET SOME MUCH NEEDED REST.

THIS BIBLE STORY IS SO IMPORTANT THAT MATTHEW, MARK, AND LUKE RECORDED IT in their Gospels.

HERE, MARK IS RECORDING THIS STORY AS IT WAS GIVEN to him BY THE APOSTLE PETER THROUGH Peter's PREACHING and teaching.

MARK SHOWS US THAT JESUS CAN DEAL, NOT ONLY WITH THE NATURAL EVILS SUCH AS THE STORMS ON THE LAKE as we saw in last week's message, BUT THAT JESUS CAN DEAL WITH THE EVIL THAT we face in life AS WELL.

WHEN JESUS GOT OUT OF THE BOAT HE WAS TRAVELING IN, JESUS AND HIS DISCIPLES MET A VERY PATHETIC MAN.

I.   LET'S LOOK AT THIS MAN.

HE WAS very much DEMON POSSESSED.

HE DIDN'T WEAR ANY CLOTHES, AND HE LIVED IN A CEMETERY AMONG THE GRAVES, IN THE LIMESTONE CAVES WHICH LINED THE CLIFFS ALONG THE EDGE OF THE SEA OF GALILEE.

HE WAS SO outcast and WILD THAT OTHER PEOPLE WERE AFRAID OF HIM.

ON SEVERAL OCCASIONS THE PEOPLE WHO LIVED IN THE TOWN OF GADARA TRIED TO BIND HIM WITH CHAINS, BUT HE BROKE THE CHAINS LIKE THEY WERE PAPER.

NO ONE HAD ENOUGH STRENGTH TO SUBDUE HIM.

HIS WRISTS AND ANKLES SHOWED THE MARKS OF THE CHAINS THAT WERE USED TO BIND HIM.

THIS SHOWS US this man's TORMENT.

HE WAS WANDERING UP AND DOWN THE MOUNTAINS, CRYING OUT WITH PAIN AT THE TORMENT HE FELT WITHIN HIMSELF, BRUISING AND CUTTING HIMSELF WITH STONES, IN AN ATTEMPT TO DRIVE OUT HIS INNER TORMENT.

Can this be real?

Do demons really exist, and can they have an impact on our lives?

Well, for years those who consider themselves the intelligentsia of our society, those who believe everything can be explained in anti-supernatural terms, have told us it is not rational or scientific to believe in demons.

But times are changing.

Reports of Satanic practices and demonic activity are increasing in our Western culture.

Ritualistic killings are being liked to Satanism — from the Night Stalker slayings of Richard Ramirez to the drug-cult murders in Matamoros, Mexico.

Tom Fennell, writing in Macleans magazine says that " . . . across North America, a growing number of respected mental-health therapists have come to the chilling conclusion that the tormented ravings of patients who claim to have been sexually abused as children by members of satanic cults are true reflections of their experience."

On December 6th, 1987, in Missouri, Pete Roland, a student at Carl Junction High School, confessed to the brutal murder of Steve Newberry, another student.

He and two other Carl Junction boys had bludgeoned Steve to death, beating him with baseball bats.

Their motive - a desire to please Satan.

They said they had heard voices inside their heads urging them to kill.

They attributed these voices to Satan.

It should also be noted that they all listened to heavy-metal music, much of which contains satanic themes and they also used drugs, and alcohol, and like to watch horror movies.

But they did it for Satan, who, as Jim Hardy, one of the boys said, had promised him a surge of power for taking a human life.

Or, you might have turned on your television on April 5th, 1991 to hear ABC's 20/20 co-host Barbara Walters portentously ask, "Is the Devil real?"

It was the first-ever televised exorcism.

AS this demon possessed man in our text APPROACHES JESUS, WE SEE HIS CONDITION.

NOTICE IN VERSE 9, JESUS ASKED HIM, "WHAT IS YOUR NAME?"

HE REPLIED, "MY NAME IS LEGION, FOR WE ARE MANY."

AND IN VERSE 10, THE DEMONIAC BEGGED JESUS NOT TO SEND THEM (PLURAL) MEANING MORE THAN ONE TO THE ABYSS.

WHAT COULD HAVE BEEN WRONG WITH HIM.

WELL, HE COULD HAVE HAD A SPLIT PERSONALITY OR AN ANTISOCIAL PERSONALITY DISORDER.

Many have said that THERE IS CERTAINLY EVIDENCE HERE OF MORE THAN ONE PERSONALITY.

HE MAY HAVE SUFFERED FROM SCHIZOPHRENIA.

THERE IS ALSO EVIDENCE OF SUICIDAL TENDENCIES.

WHEN THE DEMONS WERE CAST OUT, THEY ENTERED THE PIGS, AND WHAT DID THEY DO?

ALL 2,000 OF THEM RUSHED DOWN THE MOUNTAINSIDE AND DROWNED IN THE SEA.

WE DON'T EXACTLY KNOW THE FULL EXTENT OF WHAT COULD HAVE BEEN HIS PSYCHOLOGICAL PROBLEMS, BUT WE DO KNOW THAT HE HAD SEPARATED HIMSELF FROM HIS PEERS AND HIS WORST ENEMY WAS HIMSELF.

HE HAD A HOME AND HE HAD FRIENDS, BECAUSE JESUS SENT HIM BACK TO HIS HOME AND FRIENDS AT THE END OF THE STORY.

HE WAS CONSIDERED INCURABLE AND BEYOND HELP BY HIS PEERS.

THE BIBLE SAYS THAT DEMONS, WHO CALLED THEMSELVES "LEGION" WHICH MEANS "MANY" WERE POSSESSING THIS MAN.

JESUS CAUSED THE MANY DEMONS WHO LIVED IN THIS MAN TO LEAVE HIM AND ENTER INTO A HERD OF PIGS.

THEN, WHEN THE MEN WHO HAD BEEN FEEDING THE HERD OF ABOUT 2,000 PIGS SAW WHAT HAPPENED, THAT THE PIGS "RAN AND JUMPED OFF A STEEP BANK INTO THE LAKE AND WERE DROWNED", THEY RAN AND SPREAD THE NEWS IN THE NEARBY TOWN.

THEN THE ENTIRE TOWN CAME OUT TO MEET JESUS to SEE WHAT HAD HAPPENED.

WHEN THEY ARRIVED, THEY SAW THE ONCE DEMON POSSESSED MAN, WHO LIVED IN THE CEMETERY, SITTING AT THE FEET OF JESUS, NOW CLOTHED, AND IN HIS RIGHT STATE OF MIND.

THEN, SOMETHING AMAZING HAPPENED.

THIS IS WHAT WE WOULD CALL THE SEQUEL TO THE STORY.

THE PEOPLE LIVING IN THAT AREA BEGGED JESUS TO LEAVE THEM BECAUSE THEY WERE FRIGHTENED.

IT WAS AT THAT MOMENT THAT THE MAN WHO WAS HEALED ASKED JESUS IF HE COULD GO WITH HIM.
JESUS SAID TO HIM, "GO HOME TO YOUR FAMILY AND TELL THEM HOW MUCH THE LORD HAS DONE FOR YOU, AND HOW HE HAS HAD MERCY ON YOU."

II.   THIS IS THE COMMISSION OF CHRIST.

IF GOD HAS A METHOD IT'S "GO AND TELL"

WE'RE SAVED, THEN WE'RE SENT OUT to do God's work.

JESUS WAS USING THIS healed MAN AS HIS WITNESS IN THE GENTILE WORLD WHEN HE TOLD HIM TO GO HOME TO HIS FAMILY AND TELL THEM ABOUT GOD.

THIS MAN WAS SENT TO BE A WITNESS TO TELL PEOPLE WHAT HAD HAPPENED TO HIM.

AND WHAT A STORY HE HAD TO TELL!

ONCE HE WAS A MENACE and outcast TO SOCIETY, ANGRY AND HOSTILE, YET JESUS HAD FREED HIM, AND GIVEN HIM PEACE AND JOY.

WE MAY SEE A MIRROR OF OURSELVES IN THIS DISTURBED MAN --BEATEN DOWN BY OTHERS, DIVIDED or even hostile AGAINST OURSELVES, A CIVIL WAR RAGING WITHIN OUR OWN LIVES.

SIGMUND FREUD SAID THAT THERE IS ALWAYS SOMETHING WITHIN THE PATIENT "A FORCE WHICH DEFENDS ITSELF WITH ALL ITS MEANS AGAINST HEALING AND DEFINITELY WANTS TO CLING TO THE ILLNESS AND TO THE SUFFERING."

PEOPLE MAY WANT THERAPY, SAYING THAT THEY WANT TO CHANGE, AND THEN FIGHT FOR ALL THEIR WORTH AGAINST CHANGING.

YOU SEE, SOME PEOPLE FIND SECURITY IN THE DEMONS THEY KNOW control them, AND THEY ARE AFRAID TO BE DELIVERED FROM THEM.

IN THE 7TH AND 8TH CHAPTERS OF MARK, JESUS ENTERED THE SAME REGION AROUND THE TOWN OF GADARA.

THIS TIME HE WAS WELCOMED WITH a GREAT CROWD OF PEOPLE WHO CAME TO MEET HIM.

IN FACT A GROUP OF ABOUT 4,000 PEOPLE CAME TO SEE JESUS, AND THIS GREAT CROWD OF PEOPLE WAS DUE TO THE WITNESS OF THE HEALED DEMON POSSESSED MAN, WHO ONCE LIVED IN THE CEMETERY.

HE HAD TOLD HIS FRIENDS ABOUT THE WONDERFUL THING JESUS HAD DONE IN HIS LIFE AND HOW JESUS HAD COMPASSON ON HIM.

YOU SEE, EVANGELISM IS EVERYONE'S ASSIGNMENT.

WE'RE NOT ALL CALLED TO PREACH OR TO TEACH, BUT WE CAN ALL BE A WITNESS of some kind.

ACTS 1:8 SAYS, "...YOU WILL RECEIVE POWER WHEN THE HOLY SPIRIT COMES ON YOU; AND YOU WILL BE MY WITNESS IN JERUSALEM, AND IN ALL JUDEA AND SAMARIA, AND TO THE ENDS OF THE EARTH."

I'M REMINDED OF A STORY OF A LADY WHO WAS RUNNING FOR CONGRESS IN AN IMPORTANT STATE ELECTION.

SHE TOLD HER HUSBAND, "WHEN I'M ELECTED, I'M GOING TO CLEAN UP OUR STATE."

HER HUSBAND SAID, "GOOD! WHY DON'T YOU START IN THE KITCHEN!"

THERE'S A LOT OF TRUTH IN THAT.
BEFORE WE TRY TO GO TO WORK ON OTHERS, WE SHOULD BEGIN WITH OURSELF.

BEFORE THE APOSTLE PETER TELLS US HOW TO WITNESS, HE SAID, "...SANCTIFY CHRIST AS LORD IN YOUR HEARTS."

WE LIVE IN FEAR OF HAVING OUR MASKS RIPPED OFF AND MOST OF OUR LIVES ARE BUILT AROUND KEEPING OUR DEFENSES IN GOOD ORDER SO OTHERS WON'T SEE OUR WEAKNESS.

BUT WHEN WE GIVE OUR LIFE OVER TO JESUS, HE IDENTIFIES WITH OUR PAIN IN THE SAME WAY HE DID IN OUR TEXT.

IT'S INTERESTING TO NOTE HERE IN THIS STORY THAT THE PEOPLE OF THE TOWN PLACED MORE EMPHESIS UPON THE DEAD PIGS THAN THEY DID THE MAN WHO WAS HEALED.

THE PIGS in the story HAD MORE VALUE THAN PEOPLE!

THE PEOPLE WOULD HAVE RECEIVED JESUS GLADLY IF HE HAD COME AND SIMPLY LEGITIMATIZED THEIR OWN EXISTENCE.

BUT JESUS DOESN'T WORK THAT WAY.

EVEN TODAY, WE'VE TRIED TO MAKE CHRIST THE CAPTIVE OF OUR AMERICAN WAY OF LIFE, BUT JESUS WON'T BE ACCOUNTABLE TO US THIS WAY.

WE CAN'T MANIPULATE THE CHRIST, THE SON OF GOD.

HE WON'T BE OUR CAPTIVE EITHER AS AN INDIVIDUAL OR AS A CHURCH.

MY OWN WALK WITH CHRIST CONVINCES ME OF THE PAIN OF HEARING HIS WORD.

HE CALLS MY VALUES as well as my actions INTO QUESTION EACH AND EVERY DAY.

HE'S A CONSTANT DISTURBING PRESENCE IN MY LIFE AS I RAGE AT HIS GOODNESS AND Wish SOMETIMES HE WOULD just leave ME ALONE.

I WANT TO ASK YOU SOME simple QUESITONS Today.

1.   WHAT IS THE GREATEST THING THAT HAS EVER HAPPENED
      TO YOU?

COULD THE GREATEST THING BE THE CHRIST IN YOUR LIFE.

2.   WHAT IS THE GREATEST THING ANYONE OTHER THAN CHRIST
      HAS EVER DONE FOR YOU?

COULD THAT GREATEST THING BE THAT SOMEONE SHARED CHRIST WITH YOU.

3.   WHAT IS THE GREATEST THING YOU CAN DO FOR ANOTHER
      PERSON?

COULD THAT GREATEST THING BE TO SHARE CHRIST WITH THEM.

4.   WILL YOU SHARE "THE GREATEST THING" (THE CHRIST)
      IN YOUR LIFE WITH SOMEONE ELSE?

WILL YOU ANSWER YES TO THIS QUESTION.

IF YOU WILL MAKE THIS SMALL COMMITMENT IN YOUR LIFE, THE BIBLE PROMISES THAT CHRIST IN THE PERSON OF THE HOLY SPIRIT, WILL BE IN YOU AND WILL BE WITH YOU.

Jesus instructed the man to tell his people what the Lord had done for him.

After we have been set free we are to tell others that what has happened to us can happen to them.

That is the plain implication. If Christ can set others free then He can set me free.

If Christ can set us free then He can set others free.

The Scripture says, "Whom the Son sets free; he shall be free indeed."

That is the message of encouragement we need to share with others in bondage.

And then we need to pray with them that God would set them free.

What is God saying to you today?

If you are bound, He is saying that you can be free.

If you have been delivered, He is saying that you need to become an encourager to others who need deliverance.

May God help each of us to "tell what the Lord has done for you."

WHAT JARIUS' DAUGHTER SAW, IN HER FATHER

MARK 5: 35-43

One of the name's used to describe our God is Jehovah Shammah--THE GOD WHO IS THERE,

Many homes in American are suffering from the phantom father.
The father who is not there & even in some homes even when he is there, he's not there.

To carry the title of father, also carries with it great responsibilities.

Other men though living in the family, are so absorbed by there careers that they seldom spend time with the children--the effects have & are devastating, not only to the family unit, but we see its effect in our society.

Were you aware that a decade ago, the number of murders committed by teens was approx. 1000 a year, where as today it is 4000 a year.

Some would like to blame poverty, broken homes both physical & mental abuse--but as one psychologist put it there are many that come form the same back grounds that are not committing acts of violence—

Recent reports tell us:

Because of a lack of father figures in the Home-- in the past 30 years there have been:
550% increase in violent crime
400% increase in illegitimate births
200% increase in teen pregnancies.
300% increase in teen suicide
More that 70% of all juveniles in state reform institutions come from fatherless homes.

The home doesn't need a man in the house, it needs a father!

In this portion of scripture we are told of a man by the name of Jairus, he was a religious man, a ruler of the local synagogue, but he was also a father--

v 21 one tells us that Jesus is coming back into Capernaum—
He is coming from the tombs of Gadarea-

He has delivered the possessed man--upon arriving at the shore people are eventually had been looking, waiting for him--for as he arrived, much people gathered around him.

But we now focus upon one individual--one of the rulers if the Synagogue --his position is important:

Jarius was a presiding elder of the synagogue--an assembly that included the whole community of Capernaum, his position made him one of the most prominent men of the congregation.

He was neither a teacher nor a preacher, but was responsible for the order of the synagogue service.

He was the keeper of the sacred books (which were the property of the community)--he was in a sense the president of the congregation & the administrative head of the city, The city manage so to speak.

Every service he appointed someone to lead in prayer & someone to read the scripture--if there was a visiting rabbi we would invite him to read from the scriptures & comment on them.

So here we see a man with a high social position, a man known among the people, a man of prestige & power, but a man who had a desperate need-

You will never become so powerful, so popular., that will never rise so high that problems, & troubles can not reach you.

This man's little girl, the apple of his eye, was dying

Illus. those of you that have children--you can identify the feelings that man may have felt—

The first thing I want to bring out about this man is:

1. SHE SAW HE WAS NOT ASHAMED TO SEEK OUT JESUS:

    Notice he sought out Jesus--he did not send his wife, or someone else.

    When you took on the role of a father, you also were to take on the responsibilities of the father, given to you by the heavenly father:

    Paul tells us:
    Ephesians 6:4 Fathers, do not exasperate your children; instead, bring them up in the training and instruction of the Lord.

It is the father's responsibility to teach children about God, it is not solely the mothers, it is not even the church-
Yet many mothers & churches have had to take on the responsibility, simply because the father refuses to do it:

It falls upon you to give unto your children the kind of upbringing that prepares them for living lives that are pleasing unto God.

It is the family unit, not the church that is primarily responsible for the biblical & spiritual training of the children--church & Sunday school can only assist you in your training of your children:

Let me give you some instruction:

1. Dedicate your children to God --this will cause you to realize, they are a gift from God—If you don't believe their a gift, go ask a couple that cannot have children,

2. God has placed them in your care--& you HAD BETTER HANDLE THEM WITH CARE.

   2. Teach your children to fear the Lord, & to turn away from evil, & to love righteousness. Live before God, the way you would have them live before God

   3. Protect them from ungodly influences--Satan is out to destroy them just as much as he is you & I.

   4. Establish them in church--if you see no need in faithfulness to God's house, nether will they

   Teach them to fear, & reverence God & His Name, His word, & His house--teach them they are stranger & pilgrims upon this earth--we look for a place called heaven for that is where our citizenship is--& Christ is there.

   5. Instruct them in the importance in the Baptism of the holy spirit:

   6. Teach them God has a purpose for there life-

   7. Instruct them the importance of Prayer & the Word of God--have family devotions

   8. Teach by your life, your actions, not just words --for words mean very little, if they're not applied.

   Teach them God loves them too much to reward them for disobedience

Teach them --his love is unconditional, but his promises are not

Teach them that they cannot expect God to bless them with:

Finances without Tithing
Wisdom without the Word
Freedom without Forgiveness

Victory without Accountability

Abundance without Obedience
Teach & practice it yourself.

Notice:
Jarius did not send the wife or someone to take his place--but he as the father sought out the Lord himself-

Notice -- Regardless his social position, regardless of the onlookers of the townspeople, Jarius humbly knelt before Jesus--pleading with him- -Please come, for my child is dying--

Sir--- it is all right to let your children see that you have limitations--weep with them.

Let them know there are some thing you cannot do--but show them, that you have faith in the one you say you serve, faith in the one you go to church to worship, sing about--Let them hear you calling out on the Name of the Lord, not just in church--

Fathers we must be seeker of Him --seekers for wisdom, strength, guidance-for the sake of the family

Let your children know, that you are not ashamed of the Gospel, nor the God of the Gospel

Lead them to God, walk with them in God, Experience God together--don't miss out making those kind of memories.

SHOW THEM YOUR COMMITED TO GOD, TO YOUR FAMILY

It like one preacher said, IT'S TIME FOR SOME MEN TO GET OFF THERE BLESSED ASSURANCE, & START BEING FATHERS & THE LEADERS OF THE HOME GOD INTENDED THEM TO BE.

The second thing I want you notice:
his home--

Jesus sets out following Jarius to

2. SHE SAW HE WAS NOT ASHAMED TO BRING CHRIST INTO HIS HOME:

You ask, why would this be a big deal.

We must not forget Jesus was to many in the religious crowd, a friend of sinners

There are people you work with, friends, that may not understand--but as a Christian's father, one thing that is a must for your family is, Under your roof there had better been an invitation given for the king of Glory to come & reside.

One thing our country needs today is some CHRISTIAN HOMES—

Home where Christ resides.

Homes where Christ is welcome, homes where Christ is more than a picture on the wall, but a place where his presence is acknowledged, his name is honored, his word is obeyed:

So, in this story we have a distressed father, who is described as one f the rulers of the synagogue in Capernaum.

Jarius recognized Jesus as the Miracle-Worker.

Jarius felt that Jesus' presence was needed in the home where death was evident, so he pleaded for Him to come and lay His hand on his child.

Luke tells us that this girl was his only child and she was about 12 years old.

Matthew tells us that she was already dead, but Mark and Luke record that she was at the point of death.

There is no contradiction between these accounts as each man wrote distinctly and separately from the other.

When Jesus reached the home, He encountered a group of mourners, and amid the confusion, Jesus told them that the girl was not dead, but only asleep.

The crowd then laughed at Jesus for His use of the beautiful smile of sleep for death.

You remember that Jesus said the same of his friend Lazarus, that he was not dead, but just asleep.

Luke, the physician tells us that the girl's spirit or breath returned, proving that this was a resurrection, and not a recovery from a death swoon.

As soon as Jesus touched the girl, immediately she arose, and then Jesus commanded them to give her meat to eat.

It's interesting that Jesus thought of her physical needs.

Here's the lesson: the day is not far away when the dead in Christ will respond to the same quickening voice of Jesus and a resurrection of the body will take place, and we as Christians will live forever with our Lord Jesus Christ in heaven.

The death of this girl reminds us that even children die, and because they were born in sin, they need a Savior.

And this miracle reminds us of the tremendous future with Jesus Christ in heaven, when we too will have a resurrected body that is more like His, in heaven today.

MOTIVATIONAL SERMON # 003

"TELLING OUR FRIENDS ABOUT JESUS"

MARK 8:22-25

DEAR GOD, YOUR WORD SAYS THAT WE ARE A WITNESS OF THE GOSPEL OF CHRIST. THAT WE ARE SHINING LAMPS IN THE NIGHT. MAKE OUR HEARTS PURE AND GIVE US VOICES THAT ARE CERTAIN AS WE PROCLAIM OUR WITNESS FOR YOU IN A LIFE CHANGING WORK THAT GIVES US COURAGE WITH OUR CONVICTIONS. IN JESUS NAME WE PRAY.
AMEN.

DO YOU HAVE A FRIEND, A RELATIVE, OR A CO-WORKER WHO NEEDS TO KNOW ABOUT JESUS?

IF THAT PERSON IS EVER TO KNOW ABOUT JESUS, IT WILL MOST LIKELY BE THROUGH YOUR EFFORTS.

CHANCES ARE THAT IT WAS A FRIEND WHO HELPED INTRODUCE YOU TO CHRIST.

THE MAJORITY OF THOSE PEOPLE WHO COME TO CHRIST DO SO THROUGH THE INFLUENCE OF A FRIEND.

READ MARK 8:22-25 "THEY CAME TO BETHSAIDA, AND SOME PEOPLE BROUGHT A BLIND MAN AND BEGGED JESUS TO TOUCH HIM. HE TOOK THE BLIND MAN BY THE HAND AND LED HIM OUTSIDE THE VILLAGE. WHEN HE HAD SPIT ON THE MAN'S EYES AND PUT HIS HANDS ON HIM, JESUS ASKED, "DO YOU SEE ANYTHING?" HE LOOKED UP AND SAID, "I SEE PEOPLE; THEY LOOK LIKE TREES WALKING AROUND." ONCE MORE JESUS PUT HIS HANDS

ON THE MAN'S EYES. THEN HIS EYES WERE OPENED, HIS SIGHT WAS RESTORED, AND HE SAW EVERYTHING CLEARLY."

I WANT US TO LOOK AT THE LESSONS JESUS IS TEACHING US HERE!

I.   THIS MAN'S FRIENDS BROUGHT HIM TO JESUS.

THE BLIND MAN WAS INCAPABLE OF FINDING JESUS ALONE.

HE NEEDED THE HELP OF HIS FRIENDS.

SO THEY BROUGHT HIM TO JESUS AS AN EXPRESSION OF THEIR OWN PERSONAL FAITH AS WELL AS THEIR CONCERN FOR THEIR FRIEND'S CONDITION.

THIS IS A TRUE BIBLE STORY OF A MAN WHO WAS HEALED OF A PHYSICAL ILLNESS.

THIS STORY ILLUSTRATES A GREAT SPIRITUAL TRUTH: THAT TRUE FRIENDSHIP MEANS DOING SOMETHING ABOUT THE PERSONAL NEEDS OF OTHERS.

THE BLIND MAN'S FRIENDS COULD HAVE JUST BEEN CONCERNED WITHOUT ACTING ON HIS BEHALF.

THEY COULD HAVE JUST SIMPLY PRAYED ABOUT HIS CONDITION OR THEY COULD HAVE HAD COMPASSION FOR HIM WITHOUT TAKING ANY ACTION.

BUT INSTEAD, THEY DID SOMETHING ABOUT HIS CONDITION.

AND WHAT WAS IT THEY DID?

THEY BROUGHT HIM TO JESUS!

TRUE FRIENDSHIP MOTIVATES US TO WANT TO BRING OUR FRIENDS TO CHRIST.

IN MATTHEW 11:19, THE PHARISEES SAID THAT JESUS WAS THE FRIEND OF SINNERS. THEY WERE RIGHT.

JESUS HIMSELF STATED: "I HAVE NOT COME TO CALL THE RIGHTEOUS, BUT SINNERS [TO REPENTANCE]".

JESUS PROVED HIS FRIENDSHIP WHEN HE GAVE HIS LIFE FOR US SO WE MIGHT BE SAVED.

JESUS IS THE GREATEST FRIEND YOU WILL EVER HAVE.

HE PROVED IT ON THE CROSS, AND HE PROVES IT OVER AND OVER AGAIN WHEN PEOPLE GIVE THEIR LIVES TO HIM.

II.   THIS MAN'S FRIENDS BELIEVED GOD FOR HIS HEALING.

THE BIBLE SAYS IN THIS STORY IN VERSE 22 THAT THIS MAN'S FRIENDS "BEGGED JESUS TO TOUCH HIM."

NEVER UNDERESTIMATE THE POWER OF YOUR PRAYERS.

THE BLIND MAN'S FRIENDS BEGGED JESUS TO HEAL HIM, AND CHRIST RESPONDED TO THEIR REQUEST.

YOU PROBABLE HAVE FRIENDS WHO ARE IN NEED OF JESUS RIGHT NOW.

DON'T FAIL TO REMEMBER THEM IN YOUR PRAYERS.

THEY NEED YOUR PRAYERS.

REMEMBER OUR HOMEWORK ASSIGNMENT FOR THIS PAST WEEK.

HOW MANY OF YOU HAVE WRITTEN AT LEAST THREE NAMES DOWN IN A VERY CONVENIENT PLACE SO YOU CAN REMEMBER TO PRAY FOR THEM EVERY DAY?

SOMETIMES WE FAIL TO TELL OUR FRIENDS ABOUT JESUS BECAUSE WE'RE AFRAID THEY WILL BE OFFENDED OR "TURNED OFF".

I WANT TO TELL YOU, YOU'RE NOT GOING TO OFFEND THEM BY TELLING THEM YOU CARE ABOUT THEM AND YOU CARE ABOUT THEIR SPIRITUAL WELL-BEING.

MOST PEOPLE REALLY APPRECIATE YOU CARING ABOUT THEM AND THEY DESPERATELY NEED FOR YOU NOT TO GIVE UP ON THEM.

KEEP PRAYING FOR THEM.

DON'T QUIT!

GOD WILL HONOR YOUR FAITH AND HE WILL RICHLY BLESS YOUR EFFORTS.

III.   THIS BLIND MAN'S FRIENDS CARED FOR HIS NEEDS.

MARK 8:23 SAYS, JESUS "...TOOK THE BLIND MAN BY THE HAND AND LED HIM OUTSIDE THE VILLAGE.

NOW IN THE DAY OF JESUS, IT WAS COMMON FOR A PERSON TO SEE BLIND PEOPLE WHO HAD ENCRUSTED EYES BECAUSE OF INFECTION.

THIS MAN HAD APPARENTLY BEEN BORN BLIND.

JESUS TOOK THE BLIND MAN OUT OF THE CROWD AND OUT OF THE VILLAGE SO HE COULD BE ALONE WITH HIM AND DEAL WITH HIM PERSONALLY.

OFTEN, WE MUST DO THE SAME THING.

WE MUST INVITE PEOPLE OUT OF THE NOISE OF THE EVERY DAY WORLD AND INTO OUR HOMES OR OUR CHURCH SO THEY CAN REFLECT MORE SERIOUSLY ON THEIR SPIRITUAL CONDITIONS.

WE REACH OUT TO BRING THEM INTO THE HOUSE OF GOD BECAUSE THEY ARE WELCOME HERE.

OUR CHURCH SHOULD BE A SPIRITUAL HOSPITAL TO MINISTER TO THE NEEDS OF OTHERS.

THIS MIRACLE OF THE HEALING OF THE BLIND MAN IS UNIQUE.

IT'S THE ONLY MIRACLE RECORDED IN THE BIBLE SAID TO HAVE HAPPENED GRADUALLY.

USUALLY THE MIRACLES OF JESUS HAPPENED SUDDENLY AND COMPLETELY.

BUT IN THIS MIRACLE, THE BLIND MAN'S SIGHT CAME BACK TO HIM IN STAGES.

THIS WAS A UNIQUE TWO STEP PROCESS!

THERE IS A SYMBOLIC TRUTH TO BE LEARNED HERE.

AND THAT TRUTH IS, IF A PERSON LIVES TO BE A MILLION YEARS OLD, YOU WOULD STILL GO ON GROWING IN KNOWLEDGE AND GRACE.

BECOMING A CHURCH MEMBER ISN'T THE END OF THE ROAD, IT'S JUST THE BEGINNING OF THE ROAD.

MARK TELLS US THAT JESUS PUT SPIT ON THE MAN'S EYES.

THE ANCIENT WORLD HAD A CURIOUS BELIEF IN THE HEALING POWER OF SPIT.

EVEN TODAY, WHEN YOU HURT YOUR FINGER, WHAT IS THE FIRST THING YOU WANT TO DO?

USUALLY, YOU WANT TO PUT YOUR HURT FINGER INTO YOUR MOUTH TO EASE THE PAIN.

JESUS USED A METHOD OF CURING HIM THAT HE COULD UNDERSTAND.

HE WAS DEMONSTRATING COMPASSION FOR THIS BLIND MAN'S NEEDS.

IN DEMONSTRATING HIS COMPASSION, I BELIEVE JESUS TAUGHT US THREE IMPORTANT LESSONS:

1.   FIRST, WE MUST CARE FOR OTHERS.

WE MUST BE CAREFUL NOT TO BE SELF-RIGHTEOUS AND NOT TO APPEAR BETTER THAN THOU TO OTHERS.

IF JESUS CAN LOVE SINNERS, SO CAN WE.

2.   SECOND, WE MUST BEGIN TO SHARE JESUS RIGHT WHERE OUR FRIENDS ARE IN LEADING THEM TO UNDERSTAND CHRIST.

WE MUST FIRST GET ON COMMON GROUND WITH THEM AND BUILD A RELATIONSHIP WHERE THEY ARE, NOT WHERE WE ARE.

3.   AND THIRD, WE MUST ALWAYS LEAD THEM ALL THE WAY TO THE CROSS.

WE MUST FAITHFULLY AND CONTINUALLY SHOW THEM THE WAY OF THE CROSS AND NEVER WATER DOWN THE TRUTH.

IN VERSES 23-25 "JESUS ASKED, `DO YOU SEE ANYTHING?'  HE LOOKED UP AND SAID, `I SEE PEOPLE, THEY LOOK LIKE TREES WALKING AROUND.'

"ONCE MORE JESUS PUT HIS HANDS ON THE MAN'S EYES. THEN HIS EYES WERE OPENED, HIS SIGHT WAS RESTORED, AND HE SAW EVERYTHING CLEARLY."

SOMETIMES, IT'S NECESSARY FOR US TO PRAY FOR OUR FRIENDS ONE MORE TIME.

SOMETIMES, IT'S NECESSARY TO WITNESS TO THEM ONE MORE TIME.

WE CAN'T GIVE UP ON THEM.

YOU MAY BE THE ONLY FRIEND SOME PEOPLE HAVE WHO CAN INTRODUCE THEM TO JESUS CHRIST.

DON'T LET THOSE OPPORTUNITIES PASS YOU BY!

MAY GOD HELP US TO BE FAITHFUL IN SHARING THE GOSPEL WITH THOSE WHO ARE LOST.

"PROFIT AND LOSS"
"A QUESTION FOR EVERYONE"

TEXT: MARK 8:36 "WHAT GOOD IS IT FOR A MAN TO GAIN THE WHOLE WORLD, YET FORFEIT HIS SOUL?"

THE BIBLE IS FULL OF VERY IMPORTANT QUESTIONS.

THE FIRST QUESTION IN THE BIBLE IS THE QUESTION THAT GOD ASKED WHEN HE CAME DOWN INTO THE GARDEN OF EDEN AFTER ADAM AND EVE HAD SINNED:

GEN. 3:9 "WHERE ARE YOU?"

THIS IS A QUESTION FOR EVERYONE TODAY!

WHERE DO YOU STAND?

ARE YOU LIVING FOR JESUS?

ARE YOU HEADED FOR HEAVEN?

THE SECOND QUESTION IN THE BIBLE IS:

GEN. 4:9 "THEN THE LORD SAID TO CAIN, `WHERE IS YOUR BROTHER ABEL?"

TODAY, I ASK YOU, ARE YOU INTERESTED IN YOUR FELLOW MAN?

HAVE YOU TOLD YOUR FRIENDS AND NEIGHBORS ABOUT THE SAVING GRACE OF JESUS?

HAVE YOU TRIED TO HELP THEM WITH THEIR DIFFICULTIES?

THERE IS A VERY IMPORTANT QUESTION FOUND IN THE BOOK OF JOB IN THE OLD TESTAMENT.

JOB 14:14 "IF A MAN DIES, WILL HE LIVE AGAIN?"

JESUS ANSWERED THAT QUESTION WHEN HE ROSE FROM THE GRAVE.

JESUS ANSWERED THAT QUESTION WHEN HE SAID: "BECAUSE I LIVE, YOU ALSO WILL LIVE". (JOHN 14:19)

THERE IS A VERY IMPORTANT QUESTION ASKED BY THE PHILIPPIAN JAILER IN ACTS 16:30 "SIRS, WHAT MUST I DO TO BE SAVED?"

PAUL ANSWERED HIM BY TELLING HIM TO BELIEVE ON THE LORD JESUS CHRIST AND HE WOULD FIND SALVATION.

DON'T YOU WISH THAT THE WORLD WOULD CROWD AROUND US

TODAY AND ASK THAT SAME QUESTION!

PILATE ASKED AN IMPORTANT QUESTION IN MATT. 27:22 "WHAT SHALL I DO, THEN, WITH JESUS WHO IS CALLED CHRIST?"

THIS IS A QUESTION THAT EVERY PERSON WILL HAVE TO ANSWER.

GOD GAVE HIS SON FOR OUR REDEMPTION.

AND NOW HE IS ASKING ALL OF US: "WHAT ARE YOU GOING TO DO WITH HIM?"

THE QUESTION AT THE FINAL JUDGMENT WON'T BE: "WHERE DID YOU LIVE?

THE QUESTION AT THE FINAL JUDGMENT WON'T BE: "WHAT KIND OF CAR DID YOU DRIVE?

THE QUESTION AT THE FINAL JUDGMENT WON'T BE: "HOW MUCH MONEY DID YOU HAVE IN THE BANK?"

THE QUESTION AT THE FINAL JUDGMENT WON'T BE: "HOW MANY FRIENDS DID YOU HAVE?"

THE QUESTION AT THAT MOST IMPORTANT TIME WILL BE: "WHAT DID YOU DO WITH JESUS CHRIST?"

WE COME TO THIS IMPORTANT QUESTION IN OUR TEXT: "WHAT GOOD IS IT FOR A MAN TO GAIN THE WHOLE WORLD, YET FORFEIT HIS SOUL?"

THIS IS A QUESTION OF PROFIT AND LOSS!

IT'S NOT A QUESTION OF DOLLARS AND CENTS, BUT ONE OF THE ETERNAL SOUL.

IT'S NOT A QUESTION FOR THIS WORLD ONLY, BUT A QUESTION FOR ALL OF ETERNITY.

YOU MAY GAIN FORTUNE AND FAME BUT ALL OF THESE THINGS WILL PROFIT YOU NOTHING, IF, IN GAINING THEM, YOU LOSE YOUR SOUL WHICH MUST LIVE FOREVER.

I.   NO PERSON CAN GAIN THE WHOLE WORLD!

SAM WALTON, THE FOUNDER OF WALMART AND SAM'S STORES WAS WORTH 20 BILLION DOLLARS AT THE TIME OF HIS DEATH.

HE SPLIT HIS FORTUNE WITH HIS FOUR CHILDREN AND GAVE THEM 4 BILLION DOLLARS EACH

AT ONE TIME HIS PERSONAL INCOME WAS OVER 3 MILLION DOLLARS PER DAY.

TODAY, ONLY A FEW YEARS AFTER SAM WALTON'S DEATH, WALMART AND SAM'S STORES ARE ESTIMATED TO BE WORTH OVER 70 BILLION DOLLARS.

JUST SUPPOSE HE HAD LIVED TO BE 100 YEARS OLD AND MADE 3 MILLION DOLLARS A DAY FOR ALL OF THOSE YEARS.

SUPPOSE HE COULD HAVE KEPT IT ALL.

WHEN HE WAS 100 YEARS OLD HE WOULD HAVE BEEN WORTH MORE THAN THE ENTIRE GOVERNMENT OF THE THIRD WORLD COUNTIRES.

HE WOULD HAVE BEEN WORTH A LARGE PART OF THE WORLD'S WEALTH.

JUST AFTER THE TURN OF THE CENTURY, HENRY FORD'S INCOME AT ONE TIME WAS ONE-HALF MILLION DOLLARS PER DAY.

THAT'S OVER $20,000 PER HOUR, DAY AND NIGHT.

$333.00 PER MINUTE.

$5.50 PER SECOND.

BUT MR. FORD NEVER GAINED ALL THE WEALTH OF THE WORLD.

THE MOST HENRY FORD WAS EVER WORTH AT ANY GIVEN TIME WAS 2 BILLION.

HOW MUCH IS 2 BILLION DOLLARS?

IF YOU SPENT $1,000 PER DAY FOR 5,500 YEARS YOU WOULD STILL BE A MILLIONAIRE.

WHAT I AM SIMPLY TRYING TO SHOW YOU IS THAT NO ONE PERSON CAN GAIN ALL THE WEALTH IN THE WORLD.

II.   PEOPLE WOULDN'T BE SATISFIED IF THEY COULD GAIN THE WHOLE
        WORLD.

MONEY DOESN'T SATISFY!

IF A PERSON HAS $5,000 THAT PERSON SOON WANTS $10,000.

THERE ARE MANY MULTI-MILLIONAIRES WHO ARE STILL WORKING, EVEN IN
THEIR AGE, BECAUSE THEY WANT TO AMASS MORE MILLIONS, NOT
BECAUSE THEY NEED IT TO SURVIVE, BUT BECAUSE THEY ARE NOT
SATISFIED WITH WHAT THEY HAVE.

THE BIBLE IMPLIES THAT MONEY FAILS TO BRING CONTENTMENT.

MONEY FAILS TO BUILD CHARACTER, AND IT FAILS TO BUY A PERSON'S WAY
INTO THE GATES OF HEAVEN.

NO PERSON CAN GAIN ALL THE POWER OF THE WORLD.

FAME AND POWER DOESN'T SATISFY.

WHEN ALEXANDER THE GREAT WAS 32 YEARS OLD, HE SAT DOWN AND
WEPT BECAUSE THERE WAS NO MORE TERRITORY FOR HIM TO CONQUER.

A FEW DAYS BEFORE PRESIDENT WARREN G. HARDING DIED HE WAS
SPEAKING FROM THE PLATFORM OF A TRAIN, AND HE SAID:
        "THE WORLD NEEDS MORE OF THE TENDER LOVE OF GOD. AND THERE
        HAS NEVER BEEN A BETTER RULE FOR THE CONDUCT OF MEN AND
        NATIONS THAN CHRIST'S "GOLDEN RULE."

PRESIDENT CALVIN COOLIDGE WAS SPEAKING ONE AFTERNOON AT A
CHURCH DEDICATION SERVICE AND HE SAID:
        "WE WILL NEVER HAVE REAL PEACE UNTIL WE FIND IT THROUGH
        CHRIST, THE PRINCE OF PEACE."

PRESIDENT WOODROW WILSON WAS SPEAKING TO A GROUP OF PEOPLE IN
DALLAS, TEXAS ONE SUNDAY AFTERNOON, AND HE SAID:
        "LONG AGO I LEARNED TO STAKE MY ALL ON CHRIST. I WOULD NOT
        UNDERTAKE ANYTHING WITHOUT ASKING FOR HIS GUIDANCE AND
HELP.

TODAY, WE DON'T HEAR PRESIDENTS TALKING MUCH ABOUT JESUS.

AND THE WORLD WE LIVE IN TODAY HAS FOUND ITSELF IN A CHAOTIC CONDITION.

THESE MEN OF YESTERDAY, THESE FOUNDING FATHERS OF OUR NATION WERE TELLING US THAT ONLY CHRIST CAN SATISFY THE HUMAN HEART.

WE HAVE TALKED ABOUT THE FACT THAT MONEY AND POWER DOESN'T SATISFY. AND I MUST ADD THAT PLEASURE DOESN'T SATISFY.

SOLOMON WAS THE RICHEST, THE WISEST, AND THE MOST MARRIED MAN IN THE WORLD.

YET ALL THAT HE HAD DIDN'T SATISFY HIM.

THOUSANDS OF YEARS AGO, GOD AND MAN WERE SEPARATED BY SIN IN THE GARDEN OF EDEN, AND WE WILL NEVER FIND TRUE PEACE UNTIL WE COME BACK INTO A RIGHT RELATIONSHIP WITH GOD.

III.   IF WE GAINED EVERYTHING AND LOST OUR SOUL WE WOULD BE MAKING
         A BAD BARGAIN.

IT WOULD BE A BAD BARGAIN BECAUSE OUR SOUL IS OUR MOST VALUABLE POSSESSION.

IF YOU HAD A DIAMOND WORTH $3,000 AND I OFFERED YOU A LARGER STONE IN TRADE FOR IT MADE OF CUBIT ZIRCONIUM, YOU WOULD MAKE A BAD BARGAIN IF YOU ACCEPTED MY OFFER.

SUPPOSE YOU OWNED A PIECE OF PROPERTY WORTH $100,000 AND I OFFERED YOU $5.00 FOR IT.

YOU WOULD BE FOOLISH TO ACCEPT SUCH A DEAL.

HOW MUCH MORE FOOLISH IS A PERSON WHO SELLS HIS SOUL FOR THE PLEASURES OF THIS WORLD.

NO WONDER CHRIST DIED FOR OUR SINS. ONE HUMAN SOUL IS WORTH MORE THAN ALL THE VALUABLES IN THIS WORLD.

A 72 YEAR OLD MAN STOOD ONE MORNING LOOKING OVER THE RUINS OF WHAT HAD BEEN HIS VERY PROSPEROUS BUSINESS.

A FIRE THE NIGHT BEFORE HAD DESTROYED IT ALL.

HE SAID TO A FRIEND: "I AM 72 YEARS OLD. I HAVE LOST ALL THAT I HAVE ACCUMULATED OVER THE YEARS. I WILL HAVE TO START ALL OVER AGAIN. THAT'S GOING TO BE HARD."

A YOUNG MAN OF 26 YOUNG YEARS LAY IN A HOSPITAL BED. HE SAID TO HIS FRIENDS: "THE DOCTORS TELL ME THAT I'LL NEVER WALK AGAIN."

IT WOULD BE A TREMENDOUS BLOW TO LOSE YOUR HOME OR BUSINESS IN A FIRE. IT WOULD BE MORE OF A LOSS TO LOSE YOUR HEALTH.

BUT TO LOSE ONE'S POSSESSIONS OR TO LOSE ONE'S ABILITY TO WALK WOULDN'T BE THE GREATEST LOSS.

THE GREATEST LOSS IS THE LOSS OF YOUR SOUL.

AT THE END OF YOUR LIFE, IT WON'T MATTER ABOUT YOUR WEALTH, YOUR HEALTH, OR THE CONDITION OF YOUR MIND.

THE ONLY THING THAT WILL MATTER THEN WILL BE THE CONDITION OF YOUR SOUL, AND THAT WILL DEPEND UPON WHAT YOU HAVE DONE WITH JESUS CHRIST.

IF YOU LEAVE CHRIST OUT OF YOUR LIFE, YOU'LL BE LOST FOR ETERNITY.

IV.   THERE ARE MANY OFFERS MADE FOR YOUR SOUL.

SATAN MAKES HIS OFFER FOR YOUR SOUL.

BUT ALL SATAN CAN OFFER YOU IS A FEW PLEASURES AND A LIFE WITHOUT HAPPINESS AND MEANING, AND A COLD GRAVE UNITED WITH AN ETERNITY OF SUFFERING.

WHY WOULD ANY SENSIBLE PERSON ACCEPT SUCH AN OFFER?

YET THERE ARE PEOPLE ALL OVER THIS WONDERFUL LAND OF OURS WHO ARE SELLING THEIR BIRTHRIGHT AS ESAU DID, FOR THE THINGS OF THIS WORLD.

SATAN IS WINNING THE VICTORY OVER THEM.

CHRIST ALSO MAKES HIS OFFER.

HE OFFERS TO FORGIVE YOUR SINS AND ADOPT YOU INTO THE FAMILY OF GOD.

HE OFFERS TO WRITE YOUR NAME DOWN IN THE LAMB'S BOOK OF LIFE.

HE OFFERS TO GIVE YOU PEACE AND COMFORT AND HAPPINESS.

HE OFFERS TO BE WITH YOU WHEN YOU COME TO THE DARK VALLEY OF THE SHADOW.

HE OFFERS TO TAKE YOU TO AN ETERNAL HOME OF EVERLASTING HAPPINESS.

"THOUGH YOUR SINS BE AS SCARLET, THEY SHALL BE AS WHITE AS SNOW" ISA. 1:18

HOW CAN ANYONE REJECT SUCH AN OFFER FROM A WONDERFUL SAVIOUR?

V.   LET ME TELL YOU WHY YOU SHOULD ACCEPT THE OFFER OF JESUS.

BECAUSE HE LOVES YOU!

THE MESSAGE OF JESUS TO EVERY SINNER IS: "IN SPITE OF YOUR SIN AND DISOBEDIENCE AND UNBELIEF I LOVE YOU WITH ALL OF MY HEART."

"MY ARMS ARE OPEN WIDE TO RECEIVE YOU AND FORGIVE YOU AND GIVE YOU THE BEST I HAVE ON EARTH AND IN HEAVEN."

GO WITH ME FOR A MOMENT TO THE CROSS OF CALVARY!

JESUS IS DYING ON THAT CROSS FOR YOU.

IF YOU HAD BEEN THE ONLY LOST PERSON IN THE WORLD, JESUS WOULD HAVE GLADLY DIED JUST FOR YOU.

ARE YOU WILLING TO TURN YOUR BACK UPON THIS UNCONDITIONAL LOVE THAT HE HAS SACRIFICED FOR YOU?

WE ARE ALL GOING TO NEED JESUS SOMEDAY!

WE'RE GOING TO NEED HIM IN LIFE. LIFE ISN'T ALWAYS SMOOTH.

THE ROAD GETS BUMPY SOMETIMES, AND WE'RE GOING TO NEED THE HELP AND THE STRENGTH AND THE COMFORT THAT ONLY JESUS CAN GIVE.

WE'RE GOING TO NEED JESUS IN OUR DEATH.

WE'RE GOING TO NEED JESUS AT THE GREAT JUDGMENT.

WITHOUT HIM, WE ARE ETERNALLY LOST.

WITHOUT HIM WE HAVE NO HOPE.

YOU MAY BE A VERY GOOD PERSON.

YOU MAY LOVE THE BIBLE.

YOU MAY BELIEVE IN PRAYER.

BUT IF YOU DON'T KNOW JESUS CHRIST, IF YOU HAVEN'T BEEN BORN AGAIN, YOU'RE JUST PLAIN LOST, AND THAT'S ALL THERE IS TO IT.

THANK GOD, THERES HOPE IN JESUS!

ACTS 4:12 SAYS: "SALVATION IS FOUND IN NO ONE ELSE, FOR THERE IS NO OTHER NAME UNDER HEAVEN GIVEN TO MEN BY WHICH WE MUST BE SAVED."

JESUS IS OUR HOPE!
JESUS IS OUR ONLY HOPE!

ONE DAY A PASTOR MET A LITTLE BOY OUT IN FRONT OF THE CHURCH.

THE BOY WAS CARRYING A RUSTY BIRD CAGE IN HIS HANDS AND SEVERAL LITTLE BIRDS WERE FLUTTERING AROUND ON THE BOTTOM OF THE CAGE.

THE PASTOR SAID: "SON, WHERE DID YOU GET THOSE BIRDS?"

THE BOY ANSWERED: "I TRAPPED THEM OUT IN THE FIELD."

"WHAT ARE YOU GOING TO DO WITH THEM," THE PREACHER ASKED.

"I'M GOING TO TAKE THEM HOME AND PLAY WITH THEM AND HAVE SOME FUN WITH THEM, AND THEN I GUESS I'LL FEED THEM TO AN OLD CAT WE HAVE AROUND THE HOUSE."

THEN THE PASTOR ASKED THE BOY HOW MUCH HE WOULD TAKE FOR THE BIRDS AND THE BOY ANSWERED: "MISTER, YOU DON'T WANT THESE BIRDS. THEY'RE JUST LITTLE OLD FIELD BIRDS THAT CAN'T EVEN SING."

THE PASTOR SAID: "I'LL GIVE YOU $5.00 FOR THE CAGE AND THE BIRDS."

"ALL RIGHT," SAID THE BOY, "IT'S A DEAL, BUT YOU'RE MAKING A BAD BARGAIN."

THE DEAL WAS MADE. THE BOY WAS HAPPY! THE PASTOR WAS HAPPY!

THE PASTOR TOOK THE CAGE BEHIND HIS CHURCH AND OPENED THE DOOR OF THE CAGE AND THE BIRDS FLEW OUT SINGING AS THEY WENT.

THE NEXT SUNDAY THE PASTOR TOOK THE EMPTY BIRD CAGE TO THE PULPIT TO USE IT AS AN ILLUSTRATION IN HIS SERMON.

HE TOLD HIS CONGREGATION ALL ABOUT THE LITTLE BOY AND WHAT HAD HAPPENED TO THE BIRDS.

HE SAID, "THE LITTLE BOY SAID THAT THE BIRDS COULDN'T SING, BUT WHEN I RELEASED THEM FROM THE CAGE THEY WENT SINGING AWAY AND IT SEEMED AS IF THEY WERE SINGING, `REDEEMED, REDEEMED, REDEEMED."

YOU AND I ARE LIKE THOSE LITTLE BIRDS.

WE'RE IN A CAGE OF SIN.

BUT JESUS WENT TO THE CROSS AND PAID THE PRICE FOR OUR REDEMPTION.

NOW, WHEN WE COME TO HIM IN SIMPLE FAITH, WE TOO CAN SING: "REDEEMED, REDEEMED, REDEEMED, THANK GOD I'VE BEEN REDEEMED."

IT WILL PROFIT YOU NOTHING IF YOU GAIN THE WHOLE WORLD AND LOSE YOUR SOUL.

BUT IT WILL PROFIT YOU EVERYTHING IN THIS LIFE AND IN THE LIFE TO COME IF YOU WILL ONLY RECEIVE JESUS AS YOUR LORD AND SAVIOUR.

WHY NOT COME TO HIM NOW?

GOD WE STRIVE FOR TOTAL COMMITMENT
TO YOU. HELP US TO BE COMMITTED TO OUR
PLANS AS WELL AS OUR DEEDS. GRANT US A
VISION HERE IN OUR CHURCH AND PROVIDE FOR
OUR NEEDS AS WE FULFILL THAT VISION IN
YOUR NAME. HELP US AS A CHURCH TO COMMIT
TO YOUR PURPOSE. IT HUMBLES US TO SEE HOW
LITTLE WE CAN ACCOMPLISH WITHOUT YOU AND
HOW ABSOLUTELY DEPENDENT WE ARE UPON YOU.

GRANT US AS A CHURCH THAT WE WOULD
HAVE YOUR KINGDOM VISION AND LIVE IN
ACCORDANCE TO YOUR WILL. HELP US TO SEE
WHAT YOU WOULD HAVE US BECOME AS A CHURCH
WITH RENEWED COMMITMENTS DEAR GOD, YOU ARE
SO GOOD TO US AND WE THANK YOU FOR EVERY
GRACIOUS AND KIND ACT YOU SHOW US. WE
THANK YOU FOR ALLOWING US TO SHARE YOUR
LOVE BY MINISTERING TO THE NEEDS OF
OTHERS. WE PRAISE YOU FOR YOUR MERCY
AND YOUR GRACE AND YOUR LOVE FOR US AND
IN THE NAME OF OUR LORD JESUS CHRIST WE
WILL CONTINUE TO PRAISE AND WORSHIP YOU.

AMEN.

SERMON # 693

"NOTHING BUT LEAVES"
(THE PARABLE OF THE BARREN FIG TREE)

READ MARK 11:11-22

GOD IS ALWAYS LOOKING FOR SPIRITUAL FRUIT AND SPIRITUAL FRUIT IS
VERY SCARCE IN OUR WORLD.

JESUS PUT IT THIS WAY: "...BY THEIR FRUITS YOU WILL RECOGNIZE THEM."
(MATT. 7:20).

OUR CHRISTIAN JOURNEY BEGINS WITH FACTS.

WE FIRST LEARN THE FACT OF OUR SIN AND THE FACT OF GOD'S GRACE FOR
US.

WE THEN RESPOND TO THESE FACTS WITH OUR FAITH.

IN OTHER WORDS, WE TRUST JESUS AS OUR SAVIOR. THIS IS THE FAITH PART.

THEN COMES THE INNER FEELINGS OF JOY AND PEACE.

SOME PEOPLE DELAY BECOMING CHRISTIANS BECAUSE THEY ARE ALWAYS WAITING FOR A SPECIAL FEELING THAT NEVER COMES.

THEN AFTER THE JOY AND THE PEACE OF BECOMING A CHRISTIAN, THERE IS SUPPOSE TO BE THE FRUIT A CHRISTIAN PRODUCES.

THIS IS WHAT IS USUALLY REFERRED TO A "GOOD WORKS" OR "GOOD DEEDS".

EVERY NEW TESTAMENT WRITER TELLS US ABOUT THE FRUIT IN THE CHRISTIAN EXPERIENCE.

JOHN THE BAPTIST WAS THE FIRST DISCIPLE TO TELL US OF CHRISTIAN FRUIT.

HE CAME PREACHING, "REPENT, FOR THE KINGDOM OF HEAVEN IS NEAR." (MATT. 3:2).

WHEN PEOPLE RESPONDED TO HIS INVITATION AND REQUESTED TO BE BAPTIZED, JOHN THE BAPTIST DEMANDED THAT THEY FIRST BRING FORTH "FRUIT IN KEEPING WITH REPENTANCE." (LUKE 3:8).

PAUL WROTE OF THE FRUIT OF THE SPIRIT: (GAL. 5:22-23)

    LOVE   GENTLENESS
    JOY   GOODNESS   (HE TALKED
ABOUT)
    PEACE   MEEKNESS
    LONG SUFFERING   FAITH
    AND TEMPERANCE

THE FRUIT PAUL AND JOHN THE BAPTIST SPOKE OF HAD TO DO WITH ONE'S CONDUCT AND CHARACTER.

WHAT THE BIBLE EMPHASIZES ABOUT FRUIT, JESUS DRAMATIZED IN THE EXPERIENCE OF THE PARABLE OF THE BARREN FIG TREE.

READ MARK 11:11-22

THIS INCIDENT HAPPENED DURING THE LAST WEEK OF JESUS' EARTHLY LIFE.

THE WEEK BEGAN WITH THE TRIUMPHAL ENTRY INTO THE CITY OF JERUSALEM.

THIS WAS A BOLD AND DELIBERATE ANNOUNCEMENT THAT JESUS WAS THE MESSIAH AND IT WAS THE FULFILLMENT OF AN OLD TESTAMENT PROPHECY WE FIND IN ZECHARIAH 9:9.

ONCE JESUS WAS IN THE CITY OF JERUSALEM, HE WENT DIRECTLY TO THE TEMPLE.

WHAT HE SAW THERE AT THE TEMPLE DISTRESSED HIM AND SADDENED HIM GREATLY.

HE SAW A BEAUTIFUL BUILDING
HE SAW ELABORATE RITUALS
HE SAW DIGNIFIED LEADERS OF THE TEMPLE

BUT HE SAW AN ABSENCE OF REAL AND TRUE DEVOTION TO GOD.

YOU SEE, ISRAEL'S RELIGION HAD BECOME A FORM OF ORGANIZED RELIGION THAT WAS MERELY FORM AND RITUAL AND CEREMONY.

THE HOUSE OF GOD HAD BECOME A HOUSE OF EXCHANGING MERCHANDISE THAT WAS CHARACTERIZED BY EXPLOITATION AND ABUSE.

MONEY CHANGERS WERE TAKING ADVANTAGE OF THOUSANDS OF PILGRIMS WHO HAD FLOODED INTO JERUSALEM FOR THE PASSOVER.

THEY WERE CHARGING EXCESSIVE PRICES TO EXCHANGE FOREIGN CURRENCY INTO TEMPLE CURRENCY.

THOSE WHO SOLD SACRIFICIAL ANIMALS ALSO CHARGED INFLATED PRICES FOR ANIMALS THAT WOULD MEET THE PRIEST'S SPECIFICATION.

WHY, EVEN THE PRIEST THEMSELVES WERE IN ON THE EXPLOITATION AND THEY RECEIVED A KICK-BACK FROM THE PROFITS.

INNOCENT WORSHIPPERS WERE BEING GOUGED IN THE NAME OF GOD AND UNDER THE PRETENSE OF RELIGION.

THERE WAS SO MUCH BICKERING OVER PRICES IN THE COURTYARD OF THE GENTILES AT THE TEMPLE IN JERUSALEM THAT WORSHIPPERS COULD SCARCELY THINK, MUCH LESS PRAY!

GOD'S HOUSE HAD BEEN PERVERTED FROM IT'S ORIGINAL INTENDED PURPOSE.

THAT EVENING, JESUS AND HIS DISCIPLES WENT TO THE LITTLE TOWN OF BETHANY WHICH WAS ONE AND A HALF MILES AWAY FROM JERUSALEM.

THEY WENT TO BETHANY TO SPEND THE NIGHT AND GET SOME REST.

EARLY THE NEXT MORNING, AS THEY WERE WALKING BACK TO JERUSALEM, JESUS WAS HUNGRY AND READY FOR HIS BREAKFAST.

SINCE THERE WASN'T A MACDONALDS OR A HARDY'S NEARBY:

HE SAW A FIG TREE AND HE WALKED OVER TO PICK SOME OF THE FRUIT FROM THIS FIG TREE FOR HIS BREAKFAST.

THE TREE HAD ALL THE OUTWARD SIGNS OF HAVING FRUIT.

IT WAS COVERED WITH LUSH LEAVES.

BUT WHEN JESUS PUSHED BACK THE LEAVES, THERE WAS NO FRUIT.

HE FOUND "NOTHING BUT LEAVES".

WHEN JESUS SAW THIS HE PRONOUNCED A CURSE UPON THIS TREE SAYING THAT NEVER AGAIN WOULD ANYONE EAT FROM THAT PARTICULAR TREE AGAIN.

JESUS AND HIS DISCIPLES CONTINUED BACK INTO JERUSALEM WHERE JESUS CLEANSED THE TEMPLE OF THE INJUSTICES HE HAD SEEN THE DAY BEFORE.

HE TURNED OVER THE MONEY CHANGERS' TABLES AND DROVE OUT THOSE
WHO SOLD THE SACRIFICIAL ANIMALS, SAYING TO THEM, "MY HOUSE SHALL
BE CALLED THE HOUSE OF PRAYER" (MATT. 21:13).

THAT EVENING, AS THEY RETURNED TO BETHANY, THE DISCIPLES FOUND
THE FIG TREE HAD WITHERED AND EVEN DRIED UP FROM THE ROOTS.

WHEN THE ASTONISHED DISCIPLES CALLED JESUS' ATTENTION TO THE TREE,
JESUS RESPONDED BY SAYING: "HAVE FAITH IN GOD" (MARK 11:22).

THIS IS A VERY DIFFICULT STORY WE FIND HERE IN THE BIBLE.

IT'S DIFFICULT BECAUSE OF TWO THINGS.

FIRST, IT'S THE ONLY TOTALLY DESTRUCTIVE MIRACLE THAT JESUS PERFORMED.

    MANY PEOPLE BELIEVE JESUS COULDN'T HAVE DONE SUCH A THING AS DESTROY A TREE.

THE SECOND THING WE FIND THAT CAUSES US DIFFICULTY IS THAT IT WASN'T THE SEASON OF THE YEAR FOR FIGS.

THIS WAS THE PASSOVER TIME WHICH WAS THE MIDDLE OF APRIL.

THIS PARTICULAR FIG TREE MAY HAVE BEEN IN A SHELTERED SPOT, BUT NORMALLY THE FIG TREES OF THAT REGION WOULD NOT BEAR FIGS UNTIL LATE MAY OR EARLY JUNE AT THE EARLIEST.

SO EVEN IF THE PASSOVER WAS IN LATE SPRING, THE FIG SEASON WASN'T UNTIL A MONTH OR TWO LATER.

IT COULD HOWEVER HAVE BEEN POSSIBLE FOR A TREE THAT WAS SHELTERED FROM THE COLD AND WATERED REGULARLY TO HAVE SOME FRUIT EARLY.

BUT THE FRUIT WOULD CERTAINLY HAVE NOT BEEN COMPLETELY RIPE!

IN ANY CASE, THIS PARTICULAR FIG TREE GAVE AN OUTWARD APPEARANCE OF BEING A PRODUCTIVE TREE, BUT IT WASN'T.

IN A SENSE IT WAS MAKING A FALSE PROFESSION!

AND THAT'S THE REAL STORY OF THIS PARABLE.

WITHOUT BEING TOLD DETAILS, WE KNOW THAT WHAT JESUS SAW IN THAT FIG TREE WAS THE SAME THING HE HAD SEEN IN JERUSALEM THE DAY BEFORE AT THE TEMPLE.

HE SAW A COMMENTARY ON THE RELIGIOUS LIFE OF ISRAEL.

YOU SEE, ISRAEL HAD ALL THE OUTWARD APPEARANCES OF RELIGION, BUT THE PEOPLE HAD NO REAL FAITH.

THEY HAD NO COMPASSION FOR THE POOR.

THEY HAD NO MISSION TO THE WORLD.

ISRAEL'S RELIGION WAS "NOTHING BUT LEAVES".

IT WAS ALL SHOW.

IT HAD NO SUBSTANCE.

IT WAS RITUAL WITHOUT REALITY.

IT WAS WORDS WITHOUT DEEDS.

IT WAS PROFESSION WITHOUT PRACTICE.

ISN'T THERE A LESSON HERE FOR US?

WOULD THAT LESSON BE A WARNING AGAINST DISPLAYING OUR RELIGION?

WOULD THAT LESSON ALSO BE A WARNING AGAINST FALSE PROFESSIONS OR A WARNING ABOUT A RELIGION THAT BECOMES SUPERFICIAL?

THE CURSE OF THE BARREN FIG TREE IS THE CURSE OF PRESENT DAY CHRISTIANITY.

MANY PEOPLE HAVE BEEN BAPTIZED AND HAVE GONE THROUGH CONFIRMATION OF CHRISTIANITY.

THEY OBSERVE RELIGIOUS FORMALATIES AND EVEN ARE REGULAR IN CHURCH ATTENDANCE AND THEIR GIVING.

BUT THEIR RELIGION IS "NOTHING BUT LEAVES"

THE CHALLENGE HERE IS VERY CLEAR:

IF WE ARE NOT FRUITFUL, WE INVITE THE JUDGMENT OF GOD!

WHAT GOD LOOKS FOR IS FRUIT!

AND IN THE SMALL AMOUNT OF TIME WE HAVE LEFT THIS MORNING, I WANT TO GIVE YOU SOME EXAMPLES OF THE TYPES OF FRUIT GOD WANTS FROM OUR LIVES.

I.   FIRST, HE WANTS THE FRUIT OF A HOLY LIFE!

HOLINESS ISN'T AN OPTION IN THE CHRISTIAN LIFE.

IT'S AN ESSENTIAL! (IT'S BASIC).

GOD DOESN'T EXPECT US TO BE PERFECT, JUST TO BE DIFFERENT!

BE DIFFERENT IN OUR SPEECH, IN OUR VALUES, IN OUR TREATMENT OF OTHERS.

MAHATMA GANDHI READ THE NEW TESTAMENT THROUGH SEVERAL TIMES.

HE HAD THE HIGHEST ADMIRATION FOR JESUS CHRIST, THE MAN.

BUT I WANT YOU TO LISTEN TO WHAT GANDHI SAID ABOUT THE CHURCHES HE ATTENDED:

HE SAID, "I GOT THE IMPRESSION THAT THEY WERE JUST A GROUP OF WORLDLY MINDED PEOPLE GOING TO CHURCH FOR RECREATION AND CONFORMITY TO CUSTOM."

AND THEN GANDHI SAID, "I HAVE THE HIGHEST ADMIRATION FOR THE CHRISTIAN LIFE AND FOR THE CHRIST OF THE BIBLE. AND I MIGHT HAVE BECOME A CHRISTIAN IF I COULD HAVE SEEN ONE."

OH, THE WORLD DESPERATELY NEEDS TO SEE A TRUE CHRISTIAN.

THE WORLD NEEDS A FLESH AND BLOOD DEMONSTRATION OF WHAT IT MEANS TO BE A CHRISTIAN.

THE CALL OF THE BIBLE IS TO BE IN THE WORLD BUT NOT OF THE WORLD.

IF YOU AREN'T LIVING A HOLY LIFE, THERE IS A GOOD CHANCE YOUR RELIGION IS "NOTHING BUT LEAVES".

II.   SECOND, GOD WANTS THE FRUIT OF A LOVING SPIRIT.

MANY CHRISTIANS ARE "ARMPIT CHRISTIANS"

THEY CARRY A BIBLE AS BIG AS A COLUMBIA TELEPHONE DIRECTORY UNDER THEIR ARMS.

THEY ATTEND CONFERENCES AND SEMINARS AND THEY LISTEN TO CHRISTIAN TAPES AND THEY APPEAR TO BE CHRISTIAN.

BUT IT'S NOT OUR BIBLE KNOWLEDGE OR OUR CHURCH ATTENDANCE THAT MAKES US CHRISTIAN.

IT'S OUR LOVE.

IT'S SO EASY TO SLIP INTO "PHARISEEIASM".

THE PHARISEES WERE THE BIBLE EXPERTS OF THEIR DAY.

BUT THEY WERE ALSO THE MOST JUDGMENTAL, SELF-RIGHTEOUS, AND LOVELESS PEOPLE CHRIST ENCOUNTERED.

BIBLE KNOWLEDGE IS NEVER A TEST OF SPIRITUAL MATURITY.

YOU CAN'T DETERMINE WHO IS THE BEST CHRISTIAN BY A THEOLOGY TEST.

IT'S POSSIBLE TO BE STRAIGHT AS A GUN BARREL THEOLOGICALLY AND COLD AS A GUN BARREL SPIRITUALLY.

A CHRISTIAN THAT DOES NOTHING FOR OTHER HUMAN'S IN THE SPIRIT OF LOVE IS LIVING A LIFE THAT IS "NOTHING BUT LEAVES".

III.   THIRD, GOD WANTS US TO HAVE THE FRUITS OF A HUMBLE
        SERVANT.

SERVICE TO OTHERS IS THE HALLMARK OF THE CHRISTIAN FAITH.

PAUL SPOKE OF OUR SALVATION WHEN HE WROTE: "FOR BY GRACE ARE
YOU SAVED THROUGH FAITH; AND THIS IS NOT OF YOURSELVES: IT IS
THE GIFT OF GOD: NOT OF WORKS..."

BUT WHY ARE WE SAVED IN THE FIRST PLACE?

ARE WE SAVED TO SIT AND WATCH?

NO!

WE ARE SAVED TO SERVE.

AND NOT JUST TO SERVE ON A CHURCH COMMITTEE EITHER!

BUT TO SERVE THE NEEDS OF OTHERS.

SERVING ON A CHURCH COMMITTEE CAN BE, AND OFTEN IS, A SUBSTITUTE
FOR, AND AN EXCUSE FOR NOT SERVING OTHERS!

SOME CHRISTIANS KEEP BUILDING UP THEIR SPIRITUAL MUSCLES AND
THEIR KNOWLEDGE, BUT THEY DON'T USE IT FOR A GOOD PURPOSE.

IF THAT'S THE CASE, THEN OUR LIVES ARE LIKE THE BARREN FIG TREE AND
WE ARE LIVING A LIFE THAT IS "NOTHING BUT LEAVES".

IV.   FOURTH, GOD WANTS US TO HAVE THE FRUIT OF PERSONAL
       WITNESS.

A MAN WHO WAS CAUGHT IN THE ACT OF COMMITTING A SERIOUS CRIME,
APPEARED IN COURT.

THE JUDGE ASKED HIM IF HE NEEDED A LAWYER.

HE ANSWERED BY SAYING THAT WHAT HE NEEDED MOST WASN'T A
LAWYER, BUT A GOOD CREDIBLE WITNESS.

A LAWYER CAN ARGUE THE FINE POINTS OF THE LAW, BUT A WITNESS
TELLS FROM HIS OWN EXPERIENCE WHAT HAPPENED.

THAT'S WHAT GOD WANTS FROM US.

HE DOESN'T NECESSARILY NEED PEOPLE WHO KNOW AND CAN ARGUE ALL THE FINE POINTS OF THE BIBLE.

HE DOESN'T NEED PEOPLE WHO CAN ANSWER EVERY QUESTION THAT PEOPLE CAN RAISE.

WHAT GOD NEEDS IS A GOOD WITNESS!

WE CAN'T LEAVE THE WORK OF MISSIONS AND EVANGELISM TO BE DONE BY CAREER PROFESSIONALS.

WITHOUT A PERSONAL WITNESS, OUR LIVES ARE "NOTHING BUT LEAVES".

V.   AND FIFTH, GOD WANTS THE FRUIT OF OUR SIMPLE FAITH.

JESUS CLOSED OUT THE TEACHING OF THE PARABLE OF THE BARREN FIG TREE BY SAYING TO HIS DISCIPLES: "HAVE FAITH IN GOD". (MARK 11:22).

FAITH IS BY FAR THE MOST IMPORTANT FRUIT GOD WANTS FOR US.

IT'S BASIC! IT'S ESSENTIAL!

"WITHOUT FAITH IT IS IMPOSSIBLE TO PLEASE HIM."

AS CHRIST ENTERED JERUSALEM, THE PEOPLE GREETED HIM BY SPREADING BRANCHES AHEAD OF HIM THEY HAD CUT IN THE FIELDS.

THEY ALSO GREETED HIM WITH THEIR HOSANNAS.

AS JESUS ARRIVED AT THE TEMPLE, LITTLE CHILDREN FOLLOWED HIM.

THE PHARISEES CRITICIZED JESUS FOR NOT SILENCING THE CHILDREN. (MATT. 21:15).

AND JESUS RESPONDED BY SAYING: "FROM THE LIPS OF CHILDREN AND INFANTS YOU HAVE ORDAINED PRAISE?" (MATT. 21:16).

OUR BIGGEST DANGER AS CHRISTIANS IS NOT THAT WE SHALL REGARD JESUS AS UNTRUE, BUT THAT WE SHALL REGARD HIM AS UNNECESSARY IN OUR LIVES.

THE BIBLE SAYS, "BY THEIR FRUITS YOU SHALL KNOW THEM".

IF YOU'VE BEEN A DRIFTING CHRISTIAN, NOTHING FINER COULD HAPPEN TO YOU THIS MORNING THAN FOR YOU TO BECOME A 100% COMMITTED CHRISTIAN.

JESUS ASK US NOT JUST FOR OUR ADMIRATION OF HIM.

HE ASK US FOR OUR COMMITMENT!

IF YOU WILL DO THIS, YOUR LIFE WILL BEAR MUCH FRUIT!

IN JUST A FEW MOMENTS WE'LL STAND AND SING OUR HYMN OF DECISION.

OUR HEAVENLY FATHER, WE COME TO YOU THIS
MORNING TO WORSHIP WITH OUR HEARTS AND SOULS
INVESTED IN OUR CHRISTIAN FAITH.
WE KNOW THAT IT IS YOU WHO SUSTAINS US WITH
YOUR CONSTANT LOVE. FATHER, HELP US THIS DAY
TO HAVE A DAY OF RE-DEDICATION WHEN WE CAN
KNOW HOW THANKFUL WE ARE TO BE PRESENT IN THE
HOUSE OF THE LORD!

MAY WE, DEAR GOD, BE RECIPIENTS OF YOUR
RICH MERCY AND BLESSINGS AS WE ATTEMPT IN OUR
INDIVIDUAL WAYS TO SHARE WITH OTHERS. MAY WE
IN OUR GRATITUDE, HAVE THE VISION WE NEED TO
LIVE UNDER YOUR GREAT BLESSINGS IN A LAND THAT
IS FULLY ABLE TO SUPPLY OUR NEEDS. HELP US TO
APPRECIATE ALL WE HAVE IN THIS WONDERFUL WORLD
WE LIVE IN, AND TO BE PROUD OF OUR COUNTRY, OUR
COMMUNITY, AND OUR FAITH. MAY OUR CHRISTIAN
FAITH BE SEEN IN OUR FRUITS AND OUR WORKS.

THIS MORNING AS WE PRAY AND THANK YOU,
WE ASK FOR GRATEFUL HEARTS AND FOR YOUR ABUNDANT
BLESSINGS AS WE PRAY IN JESUS NAME.   AMEN.

GOOD MORNING! I TRUST TODAY YOU WILL
EXPERIENCE THE WARMTH OF OUR CHRISTIAN
FELLOWSHIP AND THE INSPIRATION OF THIS
TIME OF WORSHIP TOGETHER AS WE JOIN OUR-
SELVES IN THE PRESENCE OF GOD FOR THIS
VERY SPECIAL TIME OF WORSHIP TOGETHER.

WE'LL BE STANDING AND SINGING THE WORDS TO A BEAUTIFUL HYMN

THERE'S ONE THING I WANT TO ASK OF YOU THIS MORNING, AS WE STAND AND SING THIS HYMN TOGETHER.

FOLKS, DON'T SING IT IF YOU DON'T MEAN IT IN YOUR HEARTS!

WE'RE EXPERIENCING A REVIVAL IN THE LIVES OF OUR MEMBERS.

ASK YOURSELF THIS MORNING, FROM THE DEEPEST PLACES OF YOUR HEARTS, WHAT CAN I DO HERE AT BAYVIEW BAPTIST CHURCH TO BECOME A BETTER PERSON AND LIVE MY LIFE AS A BETTER CHRISTIAN FOR JESUS.

FOR SOME OF YOU HERE THIS MORNING, IT MAY BE THAT YOU'LL NEED TO MAKE A FIRST TIME COMMITMENT TO CHRIST, ACCEPTING HIM TODAY AS YOUR SAVIOR AND LORD FOR THE VERY FIRST TIME.

HE CAN SHOW YOU HOW REAL JOY AND PEACE CAN ENTER YOUR LIFE AND HOW YOUR LIFE CAN BE CHANGED FROM THIS DAY FORWARD.

FOR OTHERS, IT MAY BE THAT YOU JUST NEED TO RE-COMMIT YOUR LIFE TO CHRIST AND TO THIS CHURCH AND TO THIS COMMUNITY.

WE EACH HAVE SPECIAL INDIVIDUAL NEEDS.

BRING THEM TO THE ALTAR THIS MORNING AS THE HOLY SPIRIT LEADS YOU AND LEAVE HERE THIS MORNING A CHANGED AND BETTER PERSON.

Broken In Gethsemane's Shadows

Mark 14:32-52

What I do want to do this afternoon is teach you about three days in history that marked the turning of the tide in the war of all mankind, past and present.

Three days that has shaped history and eternity.

Three days spent in the shadows of the Cross.

Our journey opens in the shadows of Gethsemane where brokenness reigns.

Very late Thursday evening the week of the cross, Jesus and eleven disciples journeyed from the upper room in Jerusalem, down across the Kidron Valley.

They go upward on the side of the Mount of Olives to a Garden called Gethsemane.

The darkness of the hour reflects the darkness of this scene; for Jesus knows that Judas has gone to betray Him.

Mark 14:32-52 read now

In Gethsemane's Shadows we find…

A Place of Broken Promises – v50 – They all left Him and fled.

Remember that these are the same men who just hours before had been fighting amongst themselves over which one would be sitting at his right hand.

Men who had declared wholehearted allegiance and undying loyalty.

Peter went so far as to say – "even though all may fall away, yet I will not."

Then they left the lighted upper room where they shared the Passover – and entered the shadows of the cross.

The truth is that the world is full of broken promises.

Our commitment often falters – and our best intentions go awry.

This is how Paul talked about his struggle in the shadows. "I need something more! For if I know the law but still can't keep it, and if the power of sin within me keeps sabotaging my best intentions, I obviously need help! I realize that I don't have what it takes. I can will it, but I can't do it. I decide to do good, but I don't really do it; I decide not to do bad, but then I do it anyway. My decisions, such as they are, don't result in actions. Something has gone wrong deep within me and gets the better of me every time." (Romans 7:21-25 TMNT)

Jesus comes to us and asks couldn't you stay awake for just an hour. "Could you not keep watch for one hour?"

The ultimate broken promise walks in the shadows in the heart of Judas.

One who had walked with Jesus for so long – three years he had seen all that the other disciples had seen – but his heart was far from God.

Ambition was his god.

These men walked in the shadows of Gethsemane not because of the darkness around them but because of the darkness within them.

We walk in the shadows today not because of the darkness around us but because of the darkness within us.

Something has gone wrong deep within us, and it gets the better of us every time.

A Place of Broken Religion- Here in Gethsemane's shadows stands the Messiah of God.

And here in Gethsemane's shadows stand men blinded by Religion.

There stood the chief priests, officers of the temple, and elders – all stood blinded in their religion.

Their eyes were so blind that they see in the Savior of the world a criminal, a traitor, a blasphemer of God.

They are so blinded in the darkness that they feel a perfect hatred of the One who has come to save them.

They are so blinded in heart that they completely miss all that they have been so diligently searching for – the fulfillment of all there religious searching – the answers to all their fervent prayers.

The power of religion is to blind us from the reality of God.

Religion convinces the lost man that he is happy in his worldly surroundings.

Religion prevents the sinner from seeing the despair of his or her own soul.

Religion prevents the Child of God from understanding the love of the Father and his position in the world.

We are struck by the power of blindness and only the light of Jesus lifts the shadows of Gethsemane from our hearts and makes us see.

Only when our Religion becomes a personal Relationship do the shadows begin to recede.

A Place of a Broken Heart – And being in agony He was praying very fervently; and His sweat became like drops of blood.

That is how Luke's Gospel shares this scene with us.

How deep the darkness must have been for Jesus that night – as He fought the final battle between His humanity and His deity.

Nothing demonstrates better both the weakness of the flesh and the determination of God combined in the Messiah.

In Gethsemane's garden we see the greatest test of that challenge hurled at Jesus upon the cross – "Are you not the Christ – Save yourself and us!"

There lies the agony of this night – that one thing was impossible.

He could not save others and Himself—that is the one thing that God could not and would not do—He would not allow Himself to not go to the cross.

Here in Gethsemane's shadows the dark reality of the cross finally took shape.

Jesus weeps in the shadows of Gethsemane because His heart is broken for a people who have rejected Him.

His heart is full of the broken promises of His people – full of the broken religion of His creation – yet He kneels in Gethsemane's shadows and prays "not my will but Thine be done."

His heart broken for a broken creation – Jesus will willingly lay down His life and take it up again.

Gethsemane's shadows are the start of three days that would shake the foundations of heaven and earth in the shadows of the cross.

Prayer:

Father we stand in the shadows of Gethsemane this day – we need to see. To see the power of Your love for us. To see the power of deliverance. To know the power of sight. Remove the blindness from our eyes – and help us to see You for who You are.

Open our hearts to the One who is our Great Shepherd—the One risen from the dead, who is in heaven now, waiting for us to meet Him again. Teach us, mold us, and make us, in Jesus name we pray. Amen.

EASTER SERMON # 004

"WHEN CHRIST WAS CRUCIFIED"

READ MARK 15:20-32

WE CAN WATCH A CHILD STARVING ON T.V. AND SAY, "PASS THE BISCUITS" AND NEVER GIVE ONE DIME TO WORLD HUNGER.

WE NEED TO STOP AND TAKE NOTICE OF THE SUFFERING IN OUR WORLD.

THIS IS ESPECIALLY TRUE OF THE SUFFERINGS OF CALVARY.

CALVARY IS A VERY SPECIAL TIME AND PLACE.

FOR HERE THE SINLESS SON OF GOD HIMSELF MET SIN HEAD ON AND OVERCAME.

CAN WE DISCOVER THE DEPTHS OF GOD?

CAN WE DISCOVER THE LIMITS OF THE ALMIGHTY?

ALL THIS AND MORE CAN BE SAID ABOUT THOSE 6 HOURS CHRIST HUNG UPON THE CROSS.

THE CROSS STRETCHES UPWARD TO THE HIGHEST HEAVEN AND PIERCES THROUGH THE SIN BARRIER INTO THE BRIGHTNESS OF THE GRACE OF GOD.

THE CROSS IS A REVELATION OF SPLENDOR AND SHAME.

THE CROSS TELLS THE STORY OF PARDONED SIN AND OF SINS PUNISHMENT.

THE CROSS TELLS US THE REVELATION OF LIFE AND DEATH.

FOR THE NEXT FEW WEEKS, LEADING US INTO EASTER, WE WILL LOOK AT THE CROSS THROUGH THE EYES OF THE APOSTLES.

I.   LET'S LOOK FIRST AT THE PATHWAY TO THE CROSS.

WE CAN ONLY GUESS THE EXACT SPOT WHERE JESUS WAS CRUCIFIED.

GOLGOTHA MEANS "THE PLACE OF THE SKULL" AND SINCE THE BIBLE NEVER MENTIONS A MOUNTAIN OR A HILL, THIS COULD HAVE BEEN A SLANG NAME FOR ANY PLACE OF EXECUTION.

THERE IS, HOWEVER, A SKULL SHAPED MOUND KNOWN AS GORDON'S CALVARY JUST OUTSIDE THE OLD CITY WALLS OF JERUSALEM.

IF THIS WAS THE PLACE OF THE CRUCIFIXION, AS MANY PEOPLE BELIEVE, IT WAS ABOUT A MILE FROM THE SOLDIERS' BARRACKS.

FROM ROMAN HISTORY WE CAN GUESS THAT A SQUAD OF 5 ROMAN SOLDIERS AND THEIR CENTURIONS LED JESUS ON THE LONG ROUTE THROUGH THE CITY STREETS.

ONE OF THEM HELD UP A PLAQUE WITH HIS CRIME WRITTEN ON IT, "THIS IS JESUS OF NAZARETH THE KING OF THE JEWS".

JESUS AND THE TWO MEN CRUCIFIED WITH HIM EACH HAD TO CARRY THE HEAVY CROSS TO WHICH THEIR ARMS WOULD BE NAILED.

THE ROUTE THEY TRAVELED IS CALLED "THE WAY OF SORROW".

BUT THE PATHWAY TO THE CROSS DIDN'T BEGIN IN THE BARRACKS OF THE CRUEL SOLDIERS.

YOU HAVE TO GO BACK TO THE BIRTH OF JESUS WHEN AGED SIMEON LOOKED AT MARY AND HER BABY AND SAID TO MARY, "A SWORD WILL PIERCE YOUR SOUL" (LUKE 2:35).

YOU HAVE TO GO BACK TO THE PROPHETS AS ISAIAH SAID HE WILL BE "LIKE A LAMB LED TO SLAUGHTER" (ISA. 53:7).

YOU HAVE TO GO BACK TO THE KINGS WHEN KING DAVID SAID, "MY GOD! MY GOD! WHY HAVE YOU FORSAKEN ME?" (PS. 22).

YOU HAVE TO GO BACK TO MOSES WHO TOLD THE PEOPLE TO KILL THE PASSOVER LAMB AND SPRINKLE THE BLOOD ON THE DOOR.

THEN MOSES TOLD THE PEOPLE WHAT GOD SAID, "WHEN I SEE THE BLOOD I WILL PASS OVER YOU."

YOU HAVE TO GO BACK TO ADAM AND EVE IN THE GARDEN OF EDEN WHEN IN THEIR SIN AND SHAME, ADAM AND EVE HID FROM GOD.

AND GOD SLAUGHTERED A HELPLESS ANIMAL TO USE ITS COAT TO COVER THEIR SHAME. (GEN. CH. 3).

THIS WAS THE FIRST RECORDED DEATH IN THE BIBLE AND IT POINTED TO THE DEATH OF ALL DEATHS, WHEN JESUS SHED HIS BLOOD SO OUR SIN AND SHAME COULD BE COVERED.

BUT YOU MUST KEEP GOING BACK TO WHEN TIME ITSELF BEGAN WHEN GOD THREW THIS UNIVERSE INTO BEING, LIKE A CHILD WOULD THROW A HANDFUL OF SAND.

FOR YOU SEE, THE BOOK OF REVELATION CALLS JESUS "THE LAMB SLAIN FROM THE FOUNDATION OF THE WORLD" (REV. 13:8).

THE PATHWAY TO THE CROSS BEGAN BACK IN ETERNITY WHEN JESUS DECIDED TO DIE FOR OUR SINS.

THE DEATH OF JESUS WAS THE DECISION OF GOD AND THE SON.

HE GAVE US EVERYTHING WE NEEDED TO KILL HIM.

     THE FLIES IN HIS WOUNDS
     THE SPLINTERS OF WOOD IN HIS BACK
     THE PEOPLE WHO MADE IT HAPPEN.

HE FELT ALL THE SHAME AND PAIN WE WOULD HAVE FELT.

THAT'S WHY HE FELL BENEATH THE WEIGHT OF THE 100 POUND CROSS HE CARRIED.

THAT'S WHY HE ALMOST DIED IN GETHSEMANE AS HIS BODY WENT INTO CONVULSIONS AT THE SIGHT OF THE CUP HE WOULD DRINK IN BEING MADE SIN. (2 COR. 5:21).

HE WAS STRUCK IN CIAPHAS' HOUSE AND BEATEN LATER BY THE GUARDS.

PILATE, TO APPEASE THE JEWS HAD HIM SCOURGED.

     THIS WAS KNOWN AS "THE HALF DEATH" BECAUSE EACH LASH
     OF THE NINE-LASH WHIP, WITH PIECES OF METAL AND BONE,
     PULLED OUT MUSCLE AND SKIN.

ISAIAH SAID THEY PULLED THE BEARD OUT OF HIS FACE UNTIL HE DIDN'T LOOK HUMAN. (ISA. 50:6; 52:14).

II.   ON OUR JOURNEY THIS MORNING WE LOOK NEXT AT THE
       PEOPLE OF THE CROSS.

THE NEW TESTAMENT IS VERY SILENT ABOUT THE DEPTH OF THE PHYSICAL PAIN OF CHRIST ON THE CROSS.

IT STRESSES MORE, THE SPIRITUAL ELEMENTS, AS IT TELLS US OF THE PEOPLE WHO WERE THERE.

WE ARE ALL AT THE CROSS SPIRITUALLY, EVEN IF WE WEREN'T THERE PHYSICALLY.

HAVEN'T WE ALL RUN AWAY LIKE COWARDS FROM MANY OF THE THINGS CHRIST WOULD HAVE US DO?

1.   FIRST WE SEE SIMON.

WHEN JESUS FELL, ONE OF THE SOLDIERS COMPELLED A BYSTANDER IN THE STREET TO CARRY THE CROSS OF JESUS.

SIMON WAS FROM NORTH AFRICA AND HE WAS PERHAPS A BLACK CONVERT TO JUDAISM, IN TOWN FOR THE PASSOVER.

SIMON THE AFRICAN LATER HELPED ORDAIN PAUL AND BARNABAS IN ACTS CH. 13.

THE EVENT OF CARRYING THE CROSS OF CHRIST CHANGED SIMON'S LIFE AND MADE HIM A FOLLOWER.

HE WAS THERE BY COMPULSION.

HE HAD NO CHOICE.

2.   NEXT WE SEE THE SOLDIERS.

THE FIVE MAN DEATH SQUAD WAS THERE NOT BY CHOICE.

THEY HAD WORK TO DO AND IT WAS THE DIRTIEST WORK OF ALL.

THE UPRIGHT PART OF THE CROSS WAS PLACED IN ITS HOLE.

THE CROSS, CARRIED BY SIMON, WAS PLACED ON THE GROUND.

JESUS WAS STRIPPED NAKED, LAID ON HIS BACK ON TOP OF THE CROSS.

HIS ARMS WERE TIED TO THE BEAM AND NAILS WERE DRIVEN THROUGH THE BASE OF HIS HANDS.

THEN, THE SOLDIERS LIFTED THE VICTIM UP, ONLY A FEW FEET ABOVE THE GROUND, AND THE HORIZONTAL BEAM WAS ATTACHED TO THE UPRIGHT BEAM.

THE VICTIM'S FEET WERE CROSSED AND NAILED TO THE UPRIGHT POST.

THEN HE WAS LEFT TO HIS PAIN AND SHAME AND THE INSULTS FROM THE CROWD, AND THE FLIES, AND THE BURNING THIRST AND THE MERCY OF DEATH WHICH SOMETIMES WOULDN'T COME FOR DAYS.

THE SOLDIERS WOULD USUALLY DIVIDE THE VICTIM'S CLOTHES AMONG THEMSELVES.

THEY CAST LOTS FOR HIS COAT, HIS WAIST BAND, HIS SANDALS, HIS TURBAN, AND HIS SEAMLESS ROBE, AS PSALMS 22:16-18 HAD PREDICTED 1,000 YEARS BEFORE.

THE SOLDIERS REPRESENT THE PEOPLE WE RUB SHOULDERS WITH EVERY DAY WHO ARE CALLOUSED AND HARD.

THEY PLAY THEIR LITTLE GAMES ON THEIR WAY TO ETERNITY.

THEY COULD HAVE DONE THIS DIRTY WORK WITH MORE MERCY.

THEY COULD HAVE CALLED FOR MARY AND OFFERED HER THE PRECIOUS CLOTHES OF HER SON WHICH THEY PROBABLY SOLD FOR A FEW PENNIES.

THEY COULD HAVE, BUT THEY DIDN'T!

THEY REPRESENT THE MILLIONS WHO DIE LOST, NOT FOR THE BAD THEY DO, BUT FOR THE GOOD THEY FAIL TO DO.

3.   THIRD, WE SEE THE SENTENCED MEN.

TWO MEN WERE CRUCIFIED WITH JESUS, ONE ON THE RIGHT AND ONE ON THE LEFT.

THEY WERE PROBABLY MORE THAN "ROBBERS" (K.J.V.) BECAUSE ROBBERY WASN'T PUNISHABLE BY DEATH.

WHATEVER THEY HAD DONE, THEY DESERVED TO GO TO HELL, BECAUSE WHEN THE CROWN SNEERED AT JESUS ON THE CROSS, MATTHEW (27:44) AND MARK (15:32), TELL US THEY JOINED IN.

ISAIAH 53:12 PREDICTED JESUS WOULD BE "NUMBERED WITH THE TRANSGRESSORS."

AT HIS BAPTISM, IN LINE WITH SINNERS, JESUS IDENTIFIED WITH OUR POLLUTION AND ON THE CROSS, IN LINE WITH TWO SINNERS, HE IDENTIFIED HIMSELF WITH OUR PUNISHMENT.

ONE OF THOSE THIEVES SAW THE LIGHT, ACCEPTED CHRIST, AND WENT TO HEAVEN WITH JESUS. (LUKE 24:42).

ALL MANKIND IS SEEN ON THAT HILL.

THERE IS THE SAVIOR WHO DIED FOR SIN
THERE IS THE SAVED SINNER WHO DIED TO SIN
THERE IS THE LOST SINNER WHO DIED IN SIN.

4.   THE FOURTH PEOPLE WE SEE AT THE CROSS ARE THE
        SYMPATHIZERS.

NOT EVERYONE WAS THERE AT THE CROSS TO HATE.

THERE WERE SOME THERE TO HELP.

A GROUP OF JEWISH WOMEN TOOK PROVERBS 31:6 TO HEART.

PROVERBS 31:6 READS, "GIVE STRONG DRINK TO THE ONE WHO IS
PERISHING, WINE TO THE ONE IN BITTER ANGUISH."

THEY ARE THE FORERUNNERS OF THOSE WHO WORK IN OUR HOSPITALS,
NURSING HOMES, GHETTOS, AND ANYWHERE THERE IS A PHYSICAL NEED TO
MAKE DEATH MORE BEARABLE.

CHRIST, HOWEVER, REFUSED THE ANESTHETIC.

OUR SUBSTITUTE AND SIN BEARER WOULD NOT OMIT ONE DROP OF THE
BITTER CUP THE FATHER GAVE HIM TO DRINK FOR YOU AND FOR ME.

III.   WHAT WAS THE PURPOSE OF THE CROSS?

I LIKE TO WATCH THE T.V. SHOW CALLED "COPS".

IN NEW YORK CITY, A DESPERATE MAN STOOD ON A HIGH LEDGE DECIDING
WHETHER TO LIVE OR TO DIE.

AS THE POLICE OFFICER TRIED TO RESCUE HIM, THE PEOPLE BELOW YELLED
AND TAUNTED HIM TO GO AHEAD AND JUMP.

THIS REVEALS THE DEPRAVITY OF OUR HUMAN HEARTS AND WE SEE THIS
AT THE CROSS IN SOME OF THE BYSTANDERS.

MARK SAYS, "SOME WHO PASSED BY HURLED ABUSE AT HIM. THEY
WAGGED THEIR HEADS AND SAID, `YOU WHO WOULD DESTROY THE TEMPLE

AND REBUILD IT IN THREE DAYS -- SAVE YOURSELF AND COME DOWN FROM THE CROSS'" (MARK 15:29-30).

JESUS CHRIST COULD HAVE COME DOWN!

WHEN PETER DREW HIS SWORD IN THE GARDEN OF GETHSEMANE TO PROTECT JESUS FROM THE SOLDIERS WHO CAME TO ARREST HIM, JESUS TOLD HIM TO PUT THE SWORD AWAY.

THEN HE SAID, "DO YOU THINK I CANNOT CALL ON THE FATHER AND HE WOULD SEND ME TEN THOUSAND ANGELS RIGHT NOW?" (MT. 26:53).

JESUS COULD HAVE COME DOWN BUT HE WOULD NOT BECAUSE HE WAS THERE BY HIS OWN CHOICE.

HE WASN'T A VICTIM.

HE WAS A VOLUNTEER.

HE DIED TO ACCOMPLISH THE PURPOSES OF GOD.

HE CAME AND DIED TO REDEEM.

DON'T YOU BELIEVE HE WASN'T TEMPTED TO COME DOWN AND SMASH THAT FOUL MOUTHED CROWD!

BUT HE NEVER STOPPED LOVING THEM.

HE NEVER STOPPED WANTING TO FORGIVE THEM.

TO MOCK THE JEWS, PILATE PUT JESUS' CRIME ON A SIGN WHICH WAS NAILED ABOVE HIS HEAD.

FROM ALL THE GOSPEL ACCOUNTS WE SEE THAT THE SIGN READ: "THIS IS JESUS OF NAZARETH THE KING OF THE JEWS"

GOD USED THE PAGAN SARCASM OF PILATE TO PROCLAIM THE MAJESTY OF JESUS CHRIST.

THE SIGN, WRITTEN IN HEBREW, GREEK AND LATIN (JOHN 19:20), SHOWS HOW JESUS IS NOT ONLY THE SAVIOR OF THE WORLD, BUT THE SOVEREIGN OVER OUR WORLD.

REVELATION 19:11-16 SAYS JESUS WILL RETURN TO EARTH ONE DAY AS CONQUEROR AND ON HIS ROBE GOD WILL HAVE WRITTEN HIS SIGN, "KING OF KINGS AND LORD OF LORDS"

PAUL SAYS, ON THAT DAY, "EVERY KNEE WILL BOW AND EVERY TONGUE WILL CONFESS THAT JESUS CHRIST IS LORD, TO THE GLORY OF GOD THE FATHER" (PHIL. 2:10-11).

THE SCRIBES AND PHARISEES WILL BOW.

THE SOLDIERS WILL BOW.

THE LOST THIEF WILL BOW.

THE SAVED THIEF WILL BOW.

MARY, HIS MOTHER, WILL BOW.

I WILL BOW.

YOU WILL BOW.

THE ONLY QUESTION IS: HOW WILL YOU BOW BEFORE HIM?

WILL YOU BOW TO HIM AS YOUR JUDGE OR TO YOUR SAVIOR?

CALVARY IS A VERY SPECIAL TIME AND PLACE.

EASTER SERMON # 005

"WHEN CHRIST DIED!"

MARK 15:33-39

WHEN ADAM AND EVE REBELLED AGAINST GOD, AS WE HAVE BEEN STUDYING ON WEDNESDAY NIGHTS AT PRAYER MEETING, DEATH AND SUFFERING ENTERED THE HUMAN RACE.

GOD'S PUNISHMENT FOR OUR SIN IS SUFFERING THAT LEADS TO DEATH.

THIS IS A TERRIBLE PRICE TO PAY!

THE BIBLE SAYS, "THE WAGES OF SIN IS DEATH."

BUT, THERE IS SOMETHING GOD CAN DO AND HAS DONE FOR US.

HE CAN PAY THE PRICE FOR US.

IF WE LET HIM, HE CAN CHANGE OUR HEARTS AND LIVES IN THE PROCESS.

GOD PUT JESUS HERE AS A SACRIFICE "TO DEMONSTRATE HIS RIGHTEOUSNESS...THAT HE MIGHT BE JUST AND STILL JUSTIFY (OR PARDON) THE ONE WHO HAS FAITH IN JESUS".

THAT IS THE MEANING AS WELL AS THE MIRACLE OF THE CROSS.

THAT'S WHAT CALVARY IS ALL ABOUT!

PAYING THE JUST PRICE OR THE SENTENCE FOR OUR SINS.

ISAIAH SAID 800 YEARS BEFORE IT HAPPENED, "THE LORD HAS LAID ON HIM, THE SINS OF US ALL." (ISA. CH. 53).

I AND YOU DESERVE TO GO TO HELL FOR SOME OF THE THINGS WE HAVE DONE AND SAID.

BUT WE WON'T BECAUSE JESUS CHRIST TOOK UPON HIMSELF ALL THE PUNISHMENT.

JESUS CHRIST IS THE VIRGIN BORN GOD-MAN WHO DIED FOR OUR SINS AS NO OTHER MEMBER OF THE HUMAN RACE!

IT WAS THE THIRD HOUR, OR 9:00 IN THE MORNING WHEN JESUS WAS HUNG UPON THE CROSS.

THE FIRST THREE HOURS WERE FILLED WITH ACTIVITY.

THE LOVED ONES OF JESUS AND THE CRIMINALS WERE NO DOUBT WEEPING AND TALKING TO ONE ANOTHER.

JESUS HAD REPEATEDLY ASKED THE FATHER TO FORGIVE HIS KILLERS.

THE CROWD OF SPECTATORS HAD THEIR USUAL TRIVIAL CONVERSATIONS.

THE SOLDIERS HAD GAMBLED FOR HIS CLOTHES.

THE RELIGIOUS LEADERS HAD ASKED PILATE TO TAKE DOWN HIS SIGN, BUT HE WOULDN'T DO IT.

TO PASS THE TIME, JESUS WAS MOCKED TO COME DOWN FROM THE CROSS: FIRST BY THE SPECTATORS; THEN BY THE RELIGIOUS LEADERS; THEN BY THE SOLDIERS; AND FINALLY BY THE TWO CRIMINALS.

TIME WENT ON!

SUDDENLY, ONE OF THE THIEVES ASKED FOR PARDON AND HE RECEIVED IT.

JESUS ASKED JOHN TO TAKE CARE OF HIS MOTHER MARY AND THEN THERE WAS SILENCE AGAIN.

THEN, AT HIGH NOON, THREE HOURS INTO THE ORDEAL, WHEN THE SUN WAS AT ITS HIGHEST AND BRIGHTEST, GOD SPOKE THROUGH NATURE AND COVERED THE WHOLE LAND WITH DARKNESS.

THIS WASN'T AN ECLIPSE!

THROUGH SUPERNATURAL MEANS, GOD HID HIS SON'S SUFFERINGS AND SHAME FROM THE EYES OF THE DIRTY WORLD.

IT WAS AS THOUGH THE UNIVERSE ITSELF WENT INTO MOURNING.

WHEN JESUS WAS BORN, THE SKY LIT UP IN THE MIDDLE OF THE NIGHT WITH THE GLORY OF GOD; BUT WHEN JESUS DIED THE SKY WENT DARK IN THE MIDDLE OF THE DAY.

THE DARKNESS STAYED FOR THREE HOURS AND DURING THAT TIME NOT ONE WORD IS RECORDED.

DARKNESS IS THE BIBLE'S SYMBOL FOR SIN.

THESE THREE HOURS ARE WHEN JESUS SUFFERED SPIRITUALLY.

THESE THREE HOURS ARE WHEN HE FACED AND CONQUERED THE AWFUL THING HE DREW BACK FROM IN THE GARDEN OF GETHSEMANE.

AS PAUL PUT IT, HE WAS "BEING MADE SIN" (II COR. 5:21).

"CHRIST REDEEMED US FROM THE CURSE OF THE LAW, BY BECOMING A CURSE FOR US." (GAL. 3:13).

WE ARE SPIRITUALLY DEAD BECAUSE OF OUR DEPRAVED NATURE, UNTIL WE ACCEPT CHRIST INTO OUR LIVES.

WHEN JESUS CHRIST, WHO KNEW NO SIN, WAS MADE TO BE SIN, HE RECEIVED A DEPRAVED NATURE AND DIED SPIRITUALLY FOR YOU AND FOR ME.

AT THE NINTH HOUR (3:00 P.M.), JESUS CRIED OUT, "MY GOD, MY GOD, WHY HAVE YOU FORSAKEN ME?"

FIRST, JESUS WAS MADE SIN.

THEN HE BECAME A CURSE OR A REPROACH TO GOD.

THEN, HERE, HE DIED THE SECOND DEATH, WHICH IS SEPARATION FROM GOD.

AND RIGHT THEN AND THERE, SIN'S WAGES WERE ALL PAID FOR ANYONE WHO WILL ACCEPT THEM.

THE FATHER AND THE SON PAID THE PRICE FOR YOU AND FOR ME.

THE SON WAS SEPARATED FROM THE FATHER SO WE WILL NEVER HAVE TO BE.

THE SON PUNISHED HIMSELF SO WE WILL NEVER HAVE TO BE.

THE SON WENT TO HELL SO WE WILL NEVER HAVE TO GO!

THE LAST THING JESUS DID FOR US ON THIS EARTH WAS TO DIE PHYSICALLY.

JESUS DIED WHEN HE CHOSE TO DIE.

HIS LIFE WASN'T TAKEN, IT WAS GIVEN.

HE CHOSE THE MOMENT OF HIS DEATH.

HE WAS IN COMMAND OF THE SITUATION.

DEATH DIDN'T LAY ITS HANDS UPON HIM UNTIL HE GAVE DEATH PERMISSION.

HE DIED VOLUNTARILY AS HE "GAVE HIMSELF AS RANSOM FOR ALL" (I TIM. 2:6).

LUKE SAYS THAT JESUS SAID, "FATHER, INTO YOUR HANDS I COMMIT MY SPIRIT." (LUKE 23:46).

BUT BEFORE JESUS DID THIS, HE SAID: "IT IS FINISHED."

HE DIDN'T JUST WANT TO SAY IT, HE WANTED TO SHOUT IT.

ONE OF THE BYSTANDERS WHO HEARD HIM SAY, "MY GOD, MY GOD, WHY HAVE YOU FORSAKEN ME?" THOUGHT HE WAS CALLING ELIJAH TO HELP HIM.

THE THROAT OF CHRIST WAS DRY AND HIS WORDS WERE UNCLEAR, SO TO MOCK HIM ONCE MORE, THE BYSTANDER FILLED A SPONGE WITH WINE VINEGAR (WHICH WAS A KIND OF GATORADE) THAT THE ROMAN SOLDIERS CARRIED FOR REFRESHMENT.

THE MAN LIFTED THIS VINEGAR UP TO JESUS NOT OUT OF LOVE, FOR HE SAID, "LET'S SEE IF ELIJAH WILL COME AND HELP HIM DOWN..."

TO CLEAR HIS THROAT, JESUS TOOK THE DRINK AND THEN SHOUTED:

> TO ALL THE DEVILS IN HELL
> TO ALL THE ANGELS IN HEAVEN
> TO ALL THE DEAD OF ALL AGES
> TO EVERY MAN, WOMAN, BOY AND GIRL ON EARTH

NOT THAT (HE) WAS FINISHED, BUT THAT HIS GREAT WORK OF REDEMPTION WAS FINISHED AND THE DOOR TO HEAVEN WAS WIDE OPEN TO ANY AND ALL WHO WILL BELIEVE AND REPENT.

WHEN THE SPIRIT OF CHRIST WENT UP, GOD'S SIGNATURE OF APPROVAL CAME DOWN.

WHEN JESUS DIED, ALL HEAVEN BROKE LOOSE!

LISTEN TO WHAT HEAVEN DID!

GOD REACHED DOWN AND DID THREE THINGS!

1.   FIRST, HE TOUCHED THE HUGE VEIL IN THE TEMPLE THAT HID THE HOLY OF HOLIES FROM THE HOLY PLACE AND IT RIPPED FROM TOP TO BOTTOM.

THE VEIL WAS TORN BY THE UNSEEN HAND OF GOD.

THIS WAS GOD'S WAY OF SAYING, "IT IS ENOUGH! NO MORE PRIEST, BUT JESUS! NO MORE BLOOD, BUT HIS BLOOD!"

THE CURTAIN HUNG IN FRONT OF THE HOLY OF HOLIES, THE ONLY PLACE ON EARTH GOD WOULD CONFRONT MAN. (LEV. CH. 16).

ONLY ONE MAN, THE HIGH PRIEST, COULD GO IN THERE.

AND HE COULD ONLY GO IN THERE ONCE A YEAR, ON THE DAY OF ATONEMENT.

NOW THE CURTAIN WAS RIPPED AND ANYONE, ANYWHERE, ANYTIME, CAN GO TO GOD THROUGH JESUS CHRIST.

2.	SECOND, GOD TOUCHED THE SOUL OF THE ROUGH ROMAN CENTURION IN CHARGE OF THE DEATH SQUAD AND HE SAID, "TRULY, THIS MAN WAS THE SON OF GOD."

THIS CENTURION REPRESENTS THE MOST UNLIKELIEST CANDIDATE FOR CONVERSION.

AS A SOLDIER HE HAD BEEN WITNESS TO MANY BRAVE DEATHS.

BUT TO HIM THIS ONE WAS DIFFERENT.

HE HAD HEARD JESUS FORGIVE THOSE WHO KILLED HIM.

HE HAD HEARD JESUS PROMISE HEAVEN TO ONE OF THE THIEVES BESIDE HIM.

HE HAD HEARD HIM SHOUT "IT IS FINISHED".

HE HAD HEARD WHAT GOD SAID WHEN HE SAW DARKNESS COME AT HIGH NOON.

AND HE HAD FELT THE GROUND SHAKE BENEATH HIS FEET.

SOMEHOW, HE KNEW, DEEP IN HIS SOUL, THIS WASN'T THE DEATH OF A MAN, BUT THE DEATH OF A GOD-MAN.

3.	AND THIRD, MATTHEW TELLS US THAT GOD TOUCHED THE EARTH AND IT WENT INTO A CONVULSION, OR WHAT WE WOULD CALL AN EARTHQUAKE.

LISTEN TO WHAT HAPPENED.

"THE EARTH SHOOK, THE ROCKS SPLIT APART, THE GRAVES BROKE OPEN AND MANY OF GOD'S PEOPLE WHO HAD DIED WERE RAISED TO LIFE."

"THEY LEFT THEIR GRAVES AND AFTER JESUS ROSE FROM DEATH THEY WENT INTO THE HOLY CITY, WHERE MANY PEOPLE SAW THEM." (MATT 27:51-53) (TEV).

FOLKS, THE SON OF GOD ENTERED THE HEAVENLY HOLY OF HOLIES AND AS OUR SUBSTITUTE, HE OFFERED HIS OWN PRECIOUS BLOOD.

THANK GOD HE LOVED US SO MUCH HE SENT HIS SON TO BE OUR SUBSTITUTE AND SAVIOR.

WHAT WILL BE YOUR RESPONSE TO THIS MESSAGE THIS MORNING.

WILL YOU CHOOSE LIFE BY CHOOSING JESUS CHRIST?

THE BIBLE SAYS, "WHOEVER BELIEVES IN HIM SHALL NOT PERISH BUT HAVE ETERNAL LIFE" (JOHN 3:16B).

DO YOU KNOW THAT LOVE OF GOD THIS MORNING?

CAN YOU FEEL THAT FREEDOM GOD GIVES US THIS MORNING?

ARE YOU READY TO SERVE HIM?

FATHER, WE ARE ALWAYS LOOKING
FOR MORE FAITH IN OUR WORLD. I PRAY
THIS MORNING OUR HEARTS WILL BE RENEWED
BY THE POWER OF YOUR HOLY SPIRIT. I
PRAY OUR SOULS WILL BE SOFTENED AS WE
LOOK AT THE STORY OF THE CROSS WHEN
CHRIST DIED. I PRAY FROM THIS MOMENT
WE WILL ACCEPT YOUR FORGIVENESS AND WE
WILL BE GIVEN NEW ENERGY FOR A NEW LIFE
AS WE CONTINUE TO TRUST JESUS CHRIST AS
OUR SAVIOUR. WE COME TO YOU THIS MORNING
HUMBLY ASKING YOUR WILL TO BE DONE IN
OUR LIVES. WE ARE NOT WORTHY TO COME
TO YOUR THRONE, BUT BY THE SUPREME
SACRIFICE OF CHRIST JESUS AS OUR
SUBSTITUTE WE ARE ABLE TO BECOME YOUR
HUMBLE SERVANTS. BLESS THIS CHURCH,
TODAY, DEAR GOD, I PRAY, IN CHRIST NAME.

AMEN.

EASTER SERMON # 006

"WHEN CHRIST AROSE"

TEXT: READ MARK 15:40-16:8

THE BEST NEWS THIS WORLD HAS EVER HEARD IS THAT WHEN THE WEEPING
WOMEN WENT TO THE GRAVE OF JESUS CHRIST, WORRYING ABOUT WHO
WOULD MOVE THE STONE; THAT STONE WAS ALREADY MOVED, THE GRAVE
WAS EMPTY, AND JESUS HAD AROSE!

WHY IS THIS GOOD NEWS?

HOW CAN SOMETHING THAT HAPPENED NEARLY 2,000 YEARS AGO HAVE
ANYTHING TO DO WITH YOU AND ME?

IT HAS EVERYTHING TO DO WITH YOU AND ME BECAUSE OF WHO IT WAS
WHO DIED; WHY HE DIED; AND WHAT HAPPENED TO HIM AFTER HE DIED!

STUDY THE FOUR NEW TESTAMENT GOSPELS AND YOU'LL SEE THAT JESUS
OF NAZARETH CLAIMED TO BE GOD IN HUMAN FORM.

JESUS SAID, "THE FATHER AND I ARE ONE...HE WHO HAS SEEN ME HAS SEEN THE FATHER." (JOHN CH. 14).

JESUS CLAIMED THE POWER TO FORGIVE SIN AND HE SAID THAT ONE DAY HE WOULD COME BACK TO EARTH WITH HIS HOLY ANGELS, IN THE GLORY OF THE FATHER, AND BE THE JUDGE OF EVERY MAN, WOMAN, AND CHILD WHO HAS EVER LIVED ON PLANET EARTH.

GOD RAISED HIM FROM THE DEAD AND IN RAISING HIM, SAID, "THIS IS MY BELOVED SON!"

A KINDERGARTEN TEACHER IN A CHRISTIAN SCHOOL WAS TALKING WITH ONE LITTLE BOY AND SHE BEGAN TO RELATE TO HIM THE STORY OF JESUS' DEATH ON THE CROSS.

WHEN SHE WAS ASKED WHAT A CROSS WAS, THE TEACHER PICKED UP SOME STICKS, MAKE THEM INTO A CRUDE CROSS AND EXPLAINED HOW JESUS WAS ACTUALLY NAILED TO THE CROSS AND THEN HE DIED.

THE LITTLE BOY SAID, "OH, THAT'S TOO BAD!"

THEN THE TEACHER RELATED TO HIM HOW JESUS ROSE AGAIN AND CAME BACK TO LIFE.

THE LITTLE BOY'S EYES GOT REAL BIG AND HE SAID, "TOTALLY AWESOME!"

TODAY AS WE REMEMBER JESUS CHRIST RISEN FROM THE DEAD ARE YOU ABLE TO SAY, "TOTALLY AWESOME!"?

THE RESURRECTION OF JESUS IS GOOD NEWS!

IN THE GARDEN OF EDEN, WHEN GOD JUDGED SATAN, HE SPOKE OF THE COMING CONFLICT BETWEEN SATAN AND HIS SON. (GEN. 3:15).

SATAN WOULD HURT CHRIST BUT SATAN WOULD BE CRUSHED IN THE PROCESS.

I JOHN 3:8 SAYS, "THE SON OF GOD APPEARED FOR THIS PURPOSE TO DESTROY THE WORKS OF THE DEVIL."

ON THE CROSS, JESUS CHRIST BATTLED DEATH AND HE WON.

ON THE CROSS, LIFE MET DEATH AND LIFE WON.

ON THE CROSS, JESUS MET EVIL AND JESUS WON.

ON THE CROSS, GOOD MET EVIL AND GOOD WON!

I.   THE FIRST FACT OF EASTER IS THE TERRIBLE REALITY OF DEATH

TO HAVE A REAL RESURRECTION YOU HAVE TO HAVE A REAL DEATH.

WE ALL KNOW WHAT IT'S LIKE TO HAVE A REAL DEATH!

THE BEAUTIFUL, POWERFUL BODY OF JESUS CHRIST WENT LIMP AND LIFELESS.

HE WAS ANOTHER VICTIM OF A REAL DEATH!

THIS REAL DEATH OF CHRIST IS TOTALLY INDISPUTABLE.

LOOK AT MARK 15:44-45 AGAIN: "PILATE WAS SURPRISED TO HEAR THAT HE WAS ALREADY DEAD. SUMMONING THE CENTURION, HE ASKED HIM IF

JESUS HAD ALREADY DIED. WHEN HE LEARNED FROM THE CENTURION
THAT IT WAS SO, HE GAVE THE BODY TO JOSEPH."

PILATE, HIS SOLDIERS, AND THE JEWS MADE CERTAIN THAT JESUS WAS DEAD.

ALL THROUGH HISTORY THERE HAVE BEEN ATTEMPTS TO PROVE THAT JESUS WASN'T REALLY DEAD, BUT ALL THESE ATTEMPTS HAVE FAILED.

THE ROMAN EMPIRE EXECUTED JESUS CHRIST AND THEY SEALED HIS GRAVE STONE AND SET GUARDS OVER IT.

THE DEATH OF JESUS IS AN INDISPUTABLE FACT OF JEWISH AND ROMAN HISTORY!

THE DEATH OF JESUS CHRIST WAS ALSO INFLUENTIAL.

IN THE GLORY OF THE RESURRECTION, WE SHOULDN'T FORGET THE GLORY OF THE DEATH OF JESUS.

CHRIST DIED LIKE HE LIVED!

HE DIED WELL!

HE WAS INFLUENTIAL EVEN IN THE CROSS!

THE THIEF ASKED FOR MERCY.

THE SOLDIER CALLED HIM THE SON OF GOD.

JOSEPH AND NICODEMAS WENT TO PILATE AND ASKED FOR THE BODY.

JESUS OFFERED MERCY TO HIS MURDERERS.

HE WAS THOUGHTFUL TOWARD HIS MOTHER.

HE SHOUTED WITH VICTORY.

HE GAVE UP HIS SOUL TO THE FATHER.

ALL OF THESE ARE EXAMPLES TO US OF HOW TO LIVE AND HOW TO DIE WELL!

SO HIS DEATH WASN'T WITHOUT INFLUENCE!

THE DEATH OF CHRIST IN AND OF ITSELF IS ALSO INCOMPLETE!

IF THIS WAS THE LAST SENTENCE IN THE LIFE OF JESUS: "SO THEY TOOK HIM DOWN, WRAPPED HIM IN CLOTHS AND LAID HIM IN A TOMB...AND ROLLED A STONE OVER THE DOOR"; THEN EVIL WOULD HAVE HAD THE LAST WORD!

A LITTLE BOY WAS LOOKING AT A PICTURE OF THE CRUCIFIXION IN A STORE WINDOW.

A MAN WALKED UP AND THE BOY SAID, "MISTER, THAT'S JESUS ON THAT CROSS. THOSE ARE ROMAN SOLDIERS AT HIS FEET. THAT WOMAN CRYING IS HIS MOTHER."

THE MAN ASKED, "WHERE DID YOU LEARN ALL THAT?"

"IN SUNDAY SCHOOL," HE SAID.

THE MAN TURNED AND WALKED AWAY.

THE LITTLE BOY RAN AFTER HIM YELLING, "WAIT A MINUTE, MISTER. THAT'S NOT THE WHOLE STORY. THERE'S MORE! HE ROSE FROM THE DEAD!"

THANK GOD, THAT'S NOT THE WHOLE STORY, BUT WE HAVE THE REST OF THE STORY!

THE REST OF THE STORY IS:
II.   THERE IS VICTORY OVER DEATH!

IT OFTEN TOOK DAYS FOR CRUCIFIED VICTIMS TO DIE, USUALLY FROM EXPOSURE AND DEHYDRATION.

THE ROMANS, AS AN EXAMPLE AND DETERRENT TO OTHERS, LEFT THE BODIES ON THE CROSSES TO ROT.

THE JEWISH LAW, HOWEVER, WOULDN'T ALLOW FOR A JEW WHO WAS CRUCIFIED TO STAY THERE OVERNIGHT. (DUET. 21:22-23).

BECAUSE OF THIS AND ESPECIALLY SINCE THE SABBATH BEGAN THAT VERY NIGHT AT 6:00, THE JEWS ASKED PILATE FOR PERMISSION TO TAKE THE BODY DOWN.

THE JEWS COULD HAVE AN INNOCENT MAN FRAMED AND MURDERED, BUT THEY WOULDN'T LET HIS BODY HANG AFTER 6:00 FOR FEAR THEY WOULD DISOBEY THE BIBLE.

PILATE'S SOLDIERS SAW TO IT THAT JESUS WAS DEAD.

THE QUESTION NOW WAS WHAT WOULD HAPPEN TO THE BODY?

TIME WAS RUNNING OUT.

JESUS DIED AT 3:00 P.M. AND AT 6:00 P.M. THE JEWS COULDN'T CARRY HIS BODY BECAUSE IT WOULD BE ILLEGAL TO CARRY A BODY ON THE SABBATH.

THE SOLDIERS WOULD THROW THE BODY OF JESUS IN THE GARBAGE DUMP, BUT GOD DIDN'T LET THAT HAPPEN.

JOSEPH OF ARIMATHEA -- A HIGH RANKING OFFICIAL OF THE JEWISH SENATE, THE SANHEDRIN, AND AN OLD TESTAMENT SAINT WHO WAS "GOOD AND RIGHTEOUS" LIKE THE PARENTS OF JESUS, STEPPED FORWARD.

LUKE TELLS US THAT JOSEPH OF ARIMATHEA HAD VOTED NOT TO KILL JESUS. (LUKE 23:51).

JOHN TELLS US HE WAS REALLY A "DISCIPLE OF JESUS, BUT SECRETLY BECAUSE HE WAS AFRAID OF THE JEWS". (JOHN 19:38).

WHEN JOSEPH OF ARIMATHEA STOOD UP, NICODEMAS, WHO SERVED THE SANHEDRIN, STOOD UP TOO.

THEY BOLDLY WENT TO PILATE AND ASKED FOR THE BODY OF CHRIST.

PILATE GRANTED THEIR WISH SO THEY LOVINGLY TOOK HIS BODY DOWN FROM THE CROSS, WRAPPED IT IN STRIPS OF LINEN, AND APPLIED THE SWEET SMELLING SPICES OF MYRRH AND ALOES.

THEN JOSEPH AND NICODEMAS LEFT THE BODY BURIED IN JOSEPH'S FAMILY TOMB IN JERUSALEM, WHICH WAS A CAVE IN THE ROCK COVERED BY A HUGE STONE.

WATCHING ALL THIS, NO DOUBT WITH GRATITUDE, WERE MARY MAGDALENE AND MARY THE MOTHER OF JESUS.

THE DEATH OF JESUS REVERSED SOME ROLES.

IT SENT THE DISCIPLES RUNNING IN FEAR FOR A HIDING PLACE.

JOHN WAS THE ONLY FAITHFUL DISCIPLE WHO REMAINED AT THE CROSS.

BUT IT BROUGHT TWO SECRET DISCIPLES OUT INTO THE OPEN.

FOR JOSEPH OF ARIMATHEA AND NICODEMUS, THIS WAS A COSTLY AND DANGEROUS MOVE.

THE 100 POUNDS OF SPICES MUST HAVE COST A SMALL FORTUNE ALONE.

AND FROM THIS POINT ON, THEY WOULD BE HATED BY THEIR FELLOW SANHEDRIN MEMBERS.

AND PILATE, WHO WAS ALWAYS FICKLE, COULD EASILY HAVE ARRESTED THEM FOR TREASON AND PUT THEM TO DEATH.

BUT THEY DIDN'T CARE.

THEY STOOD UP FOR THE ONE WHO DIED FOR THEM.

MARK ENDS HIS GOSPEL WITH THE SUNDAY MORNING ANNOUNCEMENT OF THE YOUNG ANGEL.

THE WOMEN WITH THEIR SPICES WERE WORRIED ABOUT WHO WOULD ROLL THE STONE AWAY FROM THE ENTRANCE OF THE TOMB.

IT WAS BEYOND THEIR STRENGTH TO MOVE THIS HEAVY STONE.

WHEN GOD ASKS YOU OR ME TO DO SOMETHING, HE ALWAYS ENABLES US TO DO IT AND HE TURNS STUMBLING STONES INTO STEPPING STONES.

WHEN DAVID FACED GOLIATH, ALL DAVID HAD WAS A SLINGSHOT, BUT IT WAS ENOUGH, BECAUSE GOD WAS WITH DAVID.

WHEN IT COMES TO YOUR HEART, OR YOUR HOME, OR YOUR HEALTH, WHAT DOES GOD WANT?

WHATEVER IT IS, YOU CAN DO IT!

NO STONE BETWEEN YOU AND DOING GOD'S WILL IS TOO BIG FOR HIM.

THE ANGEL HAD MOVED THE STONE FROM THE TOMB AND THE ANGEL MOVED ANOTHER STONE WHEN HE ANNOUNCED, "HE HAS RISEN...GO TELL HIS DISCIPLES AND PETER..." (MARK 16:6-7).

WE NEED TO PERSONALIZE EASTER AND BE EXCITED ABOUT EASTER.

WE NEED TO LIFT JESUS CHRIST UP FROM THE GRAVE TO THE RIGHT HAND OF GOD WHERE THE WHOLE UNIVERSE IS SUBJECT TO HIM.

WE NEED TO SEE HIM WALKING BY OUR SIDE.

WE NEED TO SEE HIM LOVING US AS INDIVIDUALS IN SPITE OF OUR FAILURES.

TODAY, LET'S REMEMBER THAT JESUS CHRIST WAS BEATEN AND SHAMED AND CRUCIFIED TO MAKE PAYMENT FOR OUR SINS.

BUT LET'S ALSO REMEMBER THAT HE WAS BROUGHT BACK TO LIFE BY THE POWER OF AND FOR THE GLORY OF GOD.

THE MAIN THING WE ARE TO REMEMBER THIS EASTER DAY AND EVERY DAY IS: "JESUS CHRIST: RAISED FROM THE DEAD".

WILL YOU JOIN ME TODAY AS WE COMMIT OUR HEARTS TO THIS REALITY!

DEAR GOD, WE THANK YOU FOR THAT MORNING WHEN THE SUN ROSE OVER JERUSALEM AND YOU ROSE CHRIST YOUR ONLY SON FROM THE DEAD. WE THANK YOU FOR THE ANNOUNCEMENT OF THE ANGEL THAT THE TOMB WAS EMPTY. DEAR GOD, WE REALIZE THE FOUNDATION OF THE ENTIRE CHRISTIAN SYSTEM OF BELIEFS WOULD CRUMBLE IF IT WERE NOT FOR THE RESURRECTION OF JESUS CHRIST. AS WE HEAR THESE WORDS OF HOPE THIS MORNING, WE PRAY THAT CHRIST, AND EASTER AND THE RESURRECTION WILL HAVE A MORE ABUNDANT MEANING TO US AS YOUR RIGHTEOUSNESS IS REVEALED TO US THROUGH OUR FAITH IN CHRIST JESUS. HELP US TO REALIZE THE DEPTH OF SACRIFICE CHRIST MADE FOR ALL OF US AND HELP US TO DO YOUR WORK IN OUR WORLD AS WE SHARE TODAY IN THE GLORY OF THE RISEN CHRIST.

A:\SERMON.754

"THE BACKSLIDER"

TEXT: MARK 16:7

ALL OF US ARE INTERESTED IN SIMON PETER THE DISCIPLE BECAUSE HE'S SO MUCH LIKE US.

PETER HAD HIS UPS AND DOWNS.

WHEN WE LOOK AT HIS FAILURES, REMEMBERING HOW CLOSE HE WAS TO JESUS, WE FEEL THERE'S HOPE FOR US.

I LIKE PETER'S ENTHUSIASM.

HE WAS ALWAYS BUBBLING OVER WITH EXCITEMENT.

IF PEOPLE WILL TAKE THE KNOWLEDGE THEY KNOW ABOUT JESUS CHRIST AND BE EXCITED ABOUT JESUS, THEY CAN DO GREAT THINGS FOR GOD.

I ALSO LIKE PETER'S BRAVERY.

WE DON'T THINK HE'S SO BRAVE WHEN HE DENIES KNOWLEDGE OF, OR CONNECTION WITH JESUS.

BUT HE DID FOLLOW JESUS INTO THE PRESENCE OF HIS ENEMIES WHEN ALL THE OTHER DISCIPLES EXCEPT JOHN FLED IN FEAR.

LOOK AT THE SCENE THAT WE READ IN MARK 16:7.

THE CRUCIFIXION IS OVER AND THE THREE CROSSES ARE EMPTY.
THE WORLD GOES ON AS USUAL FOR THE PEOPLE, BUT IT HAS CHANGED FOR ONE SMALL GROUP.

THEY'RE THE DISCIPLES OF CHRIST.

THEY HAD FOLLOWED JESUS, EXPECTING GREAT THINGS FOR THEMSELVES.

YOU SEE, THEY EXPECTED JESUS TO SET UP AN EARTHLY KINGDOM AND GIVE ALL OF THEM PROMINENT PLACES IN THIS KINGDOM.

BUT NOW HE'S DEAD.

HE CAN'T DO ANYTHING FOR THEM.

SO THEY GATHER IN THE UPPER ROOM AND SOB OUT THEIR SORROW ON EACH OTHER'S SHOULDER.

PETER ISN'T WITH THEM.

HE'S ALREADY DENIED CHRIST.

NOW HE'S OUT YONDER SOMEWHERE, WEEPING HIS HEART OUT.

HE'S LONELY AND SAD AND HE THINKS TO HIMSELF, "I'LL GO FIND THE OTHER DISCIPLES, MAYBE THEY CAN GIVE ME A WORD OF ENCOURAGEMENT."

SUDDENLY A VOICE IS HEARD.

IT'S MARY MAGDALENE, THE MOTHER OF JAMES.

SHE BURSTS INTO THE ROOM AND SAYS, "I'VE SEEN JESUS. HE'S ALIVE. HE'S RISEN JUST LIKE HE SAID HE WOULD. HE SENT ME TO TELL YOU TO MEET HIM."

IMMEDIATELY ALL THE DISCIPLES EXCEPT PETER SPRING TO THEIR FEET AND RUSH OUT THE DOOR.

PETER LINGERS BEHIND THINKING THAT HE'S NO LONGER ONE OF THE DISCIPLES BECAUSE HE DENIED CHRIST.

MARY TURNS TO PETER AND SAYS, "PETER, JESUS ESPECIALLY MENTIONED YOU. HE SAID, "...TELL HIS DISCIPLES AND PETER..."

WASN'T IT WONDERFUL FOR JESUS TO REMEMBER PETER?

SO PETER RAN TO MEET JESUS.

HE WAS GIVEN NEW HOPE AND A NEW MESSAGE; AND HE BECAME THE GREATEST PREACHER OF HIS DAY.

WE HAVE A TERM THAT WE USE TO LABEL PETER DURING THE TIME PERIOD BETWEEN THE NIGHT BEFORE THE CRUCIFIXION AND MARK 16:7.

PETER'S A BACKSLIDER!

WHAT IS A BACKSLIDER?

A BACKSLIDER IS A PERSON WHO HAS GENUINELY BEEN SAVED, BUT HAS DRIFTED BACK INTO THE WORLD AND OUT OF FELLOWSHIP WITH JESUS.

WHAT I WANT TO DO TONIGHT IS TO GIVE YOU THREE SIMPLE FACTS THAT YOU CAN HOLD IN YOUR MEMORY ABOUT BACKSLIDERS.

III. FIRST, I WANT TO GIVE YOU THE CAUSES OF BACKSLIDING.

10. THE FIRST CAUSE OF BACKSLIDING IS THAT YOU HAVEN'T GONE DEEP ENOUGH WITH GOD.

A LITTLE BOY FELL OUT OF HIS BED.

WHEN HIS MOTHER PUT HIM BACK IN THE BED, SHE ASKED HIM WHY HE FELL OUT AND HE SAID, "I MUST HAVE GONE TO SLEEP TOO CLOSE TO WHERE I GOT IN THE BED."

IT'S IMPORTANT TO ALWAYS GROW IN GRACE AND GO DEEPER IN YOUR CHRISTIANITY, AND THAT'S THE FIRST CAUSE OF BACKSLIDING.

11. A SECOND REASON FOR BACKSLIDING IS THAT YOU'VE BEEN DISOBEDIENT TO THE CALL OF GOD IN YOUR LIFE.

JONAH HAD A CALL FROM GOD AND HE RAN FROM IT.

THEN HE FOUND NOTHING BUT TROUBLE AND MISERY.

GOD MAY NOT HAVE CALLED YOU TO BE A MISSIONARY, BUT HE'S CALLING YOU TO SOME HUMBLE PLACE OF SERVICE OR TO AT LEAST VISIT YOUR NEIGHBOR IN THE NAME OF CHRIST.

SO WE NEED TO BE OBEDIENT TO THE CALL OF GOD IN OUR LIVES.

12. ANOTHER REASON FOR BACKSLIDING IS THAT YOU MAY HAVE BEEN HURT BY SOME TYPE OF TROUBLE, STRESS, OR SORROW IN YOUR LIFE.

TROUBLE AND SORROW SHOULD BRING PEOPLE CLOSER TO GOD, BUT OFTEN IT HAS JUST THE OPPOSITE EFFECT ON SOME PEOPLE.

13.   ANOTHER CAUSE OF BACKSLIDING IS THAT YOU MAY
        HAVE GOTTEN INVOLVED WITH THE WRONG CROWD.

YOU DON'T HAVE TO BE A TEENAGER TO BE MIXED UP WITH THE WRONG CROWD.

I KNOW A MAN WHO IS 66 YEARS OLD AND RIGHT NOW HE'S SITTING IN LEXINGTON COUNTY JAIL FOR TRYING TO HIRE SOMEONE TO MURDER THREE PEOPLE.

MANY CHRISTIANS BACKSLIDE BECAUSE THEY LEAVE THE COMPANY OF DEDICATED CHRISTIANS AND THEY GO OUT AND ASSOCIATE WITH THE WORLD.

JESUS ASSOCIATED WITH TAX COLLECTORS AND SINNERS, BUT HE NEVER GOT DOWN ON THEIR LEVEL.

HE WENT WITH THEM TO HELP THEM.

WHEN YOU LOWER YOURSELF TO THE LEVEL OF THE WORLD, YOU DO AND GO PLACES THE WORLD GOES AND YOU'RE BOUND TO BE A BACKSLIDER.

14.   THE FIFTH CAUSE OF BACKSLIDING IS THAT
        YOU NEGLECT YOUR CHRISTIAN DUTIES.

YOU MAY HAVE AT ONE TIME BEEN FAITHFUL IN YOUR CHURCH DUTIES AND YOUR PRAYER LIFE AND BIBLE STUDY.

BUT IF YOU ALLOW OTHER THINGS TO COME BETWEEN YOU AND THESE SIMPLE CHRISTIAN DUTIES, YOU BECOME A BACKSLIDER.

I TALKED TO ONE FAMILY ONE DAY WHO I VISITED TO TRY TO GET THEM TO COME AND JOIN OUR CHURCH.

THEY SAID, "WE LIKE THE CHURCH OVER AT BAYVIEW. WE LIKE THE PEOPLE, BUT WE'VE NEVER MOVED OUR MEMBERSHIP THERE BECAUSE WE DON'T KNOW HOW LONG WE'RE GOING TO BE LIVING HERE."

I ASKED THEM HOW LONG THEY'VE LIVED HERE IN THE COMMUNITY AND THEY SAID THEY'VE LIVED HERE FOR 15 YEARS, BUT THEY DON'T KNOW WHETHER THEY'LL BE HERE PERMANENTLY OR NOT.

THINK ABOUT IT!

15 YEARS THEY COULD HAVE BEEN FAITHFUL TO OUR CHURCH.

HOW UNWISE SOME PEOPLE CAN BE!

15.   ANOTHER REASON FOR BACKSLIDING IS THAT SOME
       PEOPLE LET SOME SECRET SIN STAY IN THEIR LIVES.

A PERSON'S HAIR DOESN'T TURN GRAY OVERNIGHT.

IT'S A SLOW PROCESS.

AND SIN DOESN'T USUALLY OVERCOME US IN ONE DAY, IT'S A GRADUAL PROCESS.

THEN, FINALLY, WE EMBRACE IT.

WE HAVE TO LIVE IN THE WORLD, BUT WE DON'T HAVE TO BE OF THE WORLD.

NOW THAT WE KNOW SOME OF THE REASONS FOR BECOMING A BACKSLIDER:
II.   WHAT ARE THE CONSEQUENCES OF BACKSLIDING?

16.   THE FIRST CONSEQUENCE OF BACKSLIDERS IS THAT
       WE BEGIN TO HAVE DOUBTS ABOUT OUR CHRISTIANITY.

WE WONDER IF WE'VE REALLY BEEN SAVED.

WE BEGIN TO DOUBT SOME OF THE GREAT TRUTHS OF THE BIBLE.

THAT'S THE DEVIL'S WORK IN OUR LIVES.

HE GETS AN OPENING INTO OUR HEARTS AND OUR MINDS ARE FILLED WITH DOUBTS.

SECOND TIMOTHY 1:12 SAYS, "...I KNOW WHO I HAVE BELIEVED, AND AM CONVINCED THAT HE IS ABLE TO GUARD WHAT I HAVE ENTRUSTED TO HIM FOR THAT DAY."

17.   ANOTHER CONSEQUENCE OF BACKSLIDING IS THAT
        OUR CHRISTIAN JOY IS LOST.

THERE'S NO REAL JOY IN A BACKSLIDER'S HEART.

DAVID IN THE OLD TESTAMENT WAS A MAN WHO BROKE AT LEAST 4 OF THE TEN COMMANDMENTS AT ONE TIME.

AFTER HIS SIN HE WAS MISERABLE.

IN PSALM 32:3-4 HE SAID, "WHEN I KEPT SILENT, MY BONES WASTED AWAY THROUGH MY GROANING ALL DAY LONG. FOR DAY AND NIGHT YOUR HAND WAS HEAVY UPON ME; MY STRENGTH WAS SAPPED AS IN THE HEAT OF SUMMER."
THEN ONE DAY GOD'S PROPHET, NATHAN, CONFRONTED DAVID ABOUT HIS SIN.

DAVID QUICKLY CONFESSED HIS SIN TO GOD AND IN HIS CONFESSION HE CRIED OUT, "RESTORE TO ME THE JOY OF YOUR SALVATION AND GRANT ME A WILLING SPIRIT..." (PS. 51:12).

GOD HEARD HIS PRAYER.

HAVE YOU LOST SOME OF YOUR CHRISTIAN JOY?

REPENT OF YOUR SINS TO GOD AND HE WILL FORGIVE YOU AND RESTORE YOU TO JOY.

18.   THE THIRD CONSEQUENCE OF BACKSLIDING IS THAT
        JESUS IS BEING CHEATED IN YOUR LIFE.

IF YOUR SOUL DOESN'T FEED UPON THE BREAD OF LIFE, IT GROWS LEAN.

JESUS GAVE HIS VERY BEST FOR YOU.

HE DESERVES YOUR BEST IN RETURN.

THE BACKSLIDER CHEATS HIM AND HAS NO INFLUENCE FOR CHRIST UPON OTHERS.

SO NOW WE'VE LEARNED THE REASONS FOR BECOMING A BACKSLIDER AND ALSO THE CONSEQUENCES OF BEING A BACKSLIDER.

III.   WHAT IS THE CURE FOR BACKSLIDING?

THERE ARE THREE SIMPLE STEPS.

19.   FIRST, BREAK OFF ALL THAT'S WRONG IN YOUR LIFE.

SIT DOWN ALONE AND MAKE A THOROUGH SELF-EXAMINATION OF YOUR LIFE AS IT IS RIGHT NOW.

PROBE EVERY WORD AND THOUGHT.

THEN TEAR THE THINGS THAT ARE WRONG IN YOUR LIFE OUT BY THE ROOTS.

20.   SECOND, PRAY FOR FORGIVENESS.

THE PUBLICAN PRAYED, "GOD BE MERCIFUL TO ME, A SINNER."

THAT'S BEEN CALLED THE SINNER'S PRAYER AND IT CAN ALSO BE THE BACKSLIDER'S PRAYER.

ASK FOR GOD'S FORGIVENESS.

21.   AND THIRD, COME BACK INTO THE SERVICE OF CHRIST.

THE SOUL OF A BACKSLIDER NEEDS TO BE RESTORED TO ITS NATURAL POSITION.

THINK ABOUT SIMON PETER AGAIN.

HE ONCE THOUGHT, "NOW I'M WORTH NOTHING TO JESUS AND I NEVER WILL BE WORTH ANYTHING AGAIN."

THEN THE DAY OF PENTECOST CAME AND OVER 3,000 PEOPLE ENTERED INTO THE KINGDOM OF GOD.

WHO WAS THE GREAT PREACHER WHO CONDUCTED THE SERVICES?

IT WAS SIMON PETER.

HE WAS WORTH SOMETHING TO JESUS AFTER ALL.

MAYBE YOU THINK YOU'RE NOT WORTH ANYTHING TO CHRIST.

MAYBE YOU'VE BEEN LIVING A BACKSLIDDEN LIFE.

TELL JESUS ALL ABOUT IT AND TRUST HIM TO FORGIVE YOU.

THEN LOVE HIM AND SERVE HIM.

HEAVENLY FATHER, AS WE COME TO YOU IN PRAYER, WE KNOW IN OUR HEARTS THAT YOU ARE THE LORD OF OUR LIFE AND THE AUTHOR OF EVERYTHING THAT'S GOOD. WE HUMBLY THANK YOU FOR ALL OF YOUR BLESSINGS TO US. IN THE MIDDLE OF OUR HOPING AND SEARCHING, YOU ARE THERE. WE PRAY TODAY THAT WE WILL BE CHRISTIANS OF WIDE AND CLEAR VISIONS AS YOU LEAD US AND GIVE US THE RESOURCES WE NEED TO DO YOUR WORK. WE PRAY THAT WE WILL BE EMPOWERED TO SERVE OTHERS AS WE SEEK THE OPPORTUNITIES FOR EVANGELISM AND SPIRITUAL GROWTH HERE IN OUR CHURCH. IN JESUS NAME WE PRAY. AMEN.

There is no directory with this book. May God richly bless your personal Christian ministry, Jimmy Davis

20689840R00107

Printed in Poland
by Amazon Fulfillment
Poland Sp. z o.o., Wrocław